MAYA BLUE

"Brenda survived a remarkable journey. She has my admiration."
—Dr. Jeffrey Wigand, Big Tobacco whistleblower,
former VP of research at Brown & Williamson. Academy
Award-nominated film, *The Insider*, is based on Wigand.

"Moving at a relentless pace . . . *Maya Blue* is a harrowing
memoir about existence on the edge and living to tell about it."
—*Foreword Reviews*

"A memoir of unusual strength, resilience, resonance, and purpose. . . . At times, astonished readers will do well to stop reading
for a moment and remind themselves that the experiences of
this remarkable woman and brilliant storyteller are distilled
from real life rather than the sweeping imagination of a titan of
fiction."
—*Readers' Favorite*, Five Stars

"Brenda Coffee is the embodiment of bravery, strength, and
courage, a badass woman who teaches us to advocate for ourselves."
—Grace Kraaijvanger, founder and CEO, The Hivery

"Coffee rises to show us what it means to be resilient, to fight
for one's survival. You won't be able to put this one down."
—Laura Whitfield, author of *Untethered:
Faith, Failure, and Finding Solid Ground*

MAYA BLUE

For Josie –
stay Maya Blue Strong!

MAYA
BLUE

A Memoir of Survival

———✦———

Brenda Coffee
BRENDA COFFEE

SHE WRITES PRESS

Published 2025
Printed in the United States of America
Print ISBN: 978-1-64742-906-5
E-ISBN: 978-1-64742-907-2
Library of Congress Control Number: 2025900961

For information, address:
She Writes Press
1569 Solano Ave #546
Berkeley, CA 94707

Interior design by Stacey Aaronson

She Writes Press is a division of SparkPoint Studio, LLC.

This is a work of nonfiction. The author has drawn on personal journals, recollections, and interpretations of events, changed some of the names, and compressed the timeline or omitted details.

This memoir contains passages about mental health, substance abuse and addiction, domestic violence, unsolicited and unwanted sexual advances, and assault.

For Philip: Your story shouldn't have ended this way.

And for the readers of my blog and people everywhere:
You can survive almost anything.

Maya Blue, noun

[mī-ə ʻblü]

1: An azure blue pigment used by the cultures of pre-Columbian Mesoamerica such as the Maya and the Aztecs to paint ceramics, the carved relief figures on stone pyramids, and the bodies of human sacrifices. Because this vibrant blue color has proven immune to the passage of time, temperature, and modern solvents, it is still visible centuries later and is thought to be the strongest, most resilient pigment ever created.

2: The vibrant blue color in the center of a flame.

"She wore her scars as her best attire.
A stunning dress made of hellfire."

—T.L. Martin

PROLOGUE

IT WAS A FAIRY TALE UNTIL IT WASN'T. FOR A LONG TIME, these were the only words that came to mind when I thought about my twenties and thirties. I'd pasted over the stories of what really happened as though they were generic captions in a family photo album. "Philip," "Christmas," and "Guatemala." The titles alluded to events that were shocking and almost always dangerous, but I'd put these memories in a box and hidden them in the back of my emotional closet. A life I kept secret. One that made it hard to make friends with people who lived a more normal life. People with families, children, and conventional jobs.

Looking back, I'm amazed I survived any of it, and it makes me sad to think how close I came to losing myself. How sometimes I did things not because I wanted to—things that weren't always in my best interest—but because I wanted to please my first husband, Philip Ray.

As a child, I grew up feeling abandoned by a father who raised me like I was a boarding student at a military academy and a mentally ill mother I role-reversed with after he died. At thirteen, I abandoned myself and pretended I wasn't afraid of anything or anyone. It was the only way I could take on such a job, but it kept me from discovering who I was and what I needed. It was a pattern I followed for much of my adult life.

My second husband, James Coffee, came into my life after the fairy tale had shattered into a million unrecognizable pieces. He gave me a soft place to fall, and I told him everything. All of it, because it was time to let it go. James made me feel safe, something that up until then had been only a word in the dictionary. He gave me the courage to share my story—the trauma and the abuse—but when I did, there were people who didn't believe me. My story is a lot to take in. I get that. It's far outside the norm.

Not long ago a trusted friend told me, "Most people don't believe 95 percent of what comes out of your mouth." She was referring to a group we belonged to, one that supported me during my breast cancer, after James died unexpectedly on Christmas, and when my mother died of dementia.

At first, I was stunned by her statement. How could the people I loved think I wasn't telling them the truth? My astonishment soon gave way to months of depression. My despondency turned to anger, and I wondered why it was so difficult for them to believe someone had lived a very different life from theirs. I understood they didn't have a personal frame of reference for the life I'd led, but why, in their minds, did my journey have to be a lie?

Over the years, the readers of my popular blog have been the ones who've encouraged me to write this book. They often tell me they're amazed and inspired by my life, and how I've managed to remain strong and upbeat. "You give me the courage to face and embrace the unknown and to know there is nothing I may face that can break me." But they know only a fraction of my story. One reader left me an insightful comment that was more on target than she could have imagined: "If these are the stories you're willing to share with us, what are the ones you haven't told us?"

Writing this book has helped me embrace the parts of my-self I surrendered in order to be loved. The ones that allowed me to swallow the worst days of my life for fear of being judged, and to ignore my soul that was battered and in need of nourishment. I look back at my younger self with compassion and sometimes with my mouth agape. I've traveled a long road to get to this point, but I'm a woman who's come home to herself, and I'm grateful to be here. I'm lucky to be alive, but more than that, I'm content with where I am. It's one of the things I value most.

I've written this book for every person who's afraid to tell their story for fear they won't be believed. For the people who've been hiding in self-imposed isolation and imprisonment because their truth is inconvenient or dangerous. If these people are like me, the voluntary gag order they've charged themselves with has everything to do with the shame they fear could ensue if they spoke their truth. I know why people say, "I'm fine," when inside they're coming apart, and I'm here to tell you: No matter what, never surrender your voice.

Speaking your truth is the most valuable power you have and with it, you can survive almost anything. But before you get to the point where your strength is tested—and it will be—know with every fiber of your being that you are stronger than you could ever imagine. I hope my story gives voice to yours, but more than that, I hope it offers you strength.

PART ONE

THE SPY HOUSE
ON THE HILL

"At the end of the day, it isn't where I came from.
Maybe home is somewhere I'm going
and have never been before."

—WARSAN SHIRE

CHAPTER ONE

I'VE BEEN WATCHING HIM THROUGH THE BINOCULARS from my bedroom window. A big burly weightlifter type, wearing a short-sleeved polo shirt that looks two sizes too small for him. A few moments ago he set off the alarm inside the house when he ignored the Private Property—No Trespassing sign and did a one-handed vault over the gate at the foot of our driveway. Like jumping over one of those plastic safety gates that keep puppies and children from falling down stairs, he made it look effortless. With long purposeful strides, he hikes up the hill to the house and then takes the winding front steps two at a time.

When I open the front door, there's no, "Hi, my name is . . ." He skips the niceties and gets straight to the point.

"I have it on good authority that whoever lives here needs a bodyguard." He pauses long enough for the full measure of what he said to register and then adds, "And they better watch their step." His voice is even and well-modulated, with no hint of the implied threat he just delivered, and his eyes drill into mine like he has every right to be here.

Up close, he's taller than I first thought, and his chest and upper arms look as though they're straining to break free from his shirt. He's an exaggerated muscle man clothed in preppy orange sherbet with a tiny polo player on his chest.

My first inclination is to ask how he knows we need a body-guard. Instead, I swallow the urge to engage him in conversation. This is the kind of moment I'm good at. Pretending I'm fine and not afraid of anything when I'm not fine. Dubious skills I've raised to an art form.

In a tone as calm as his, I look at him and say, "You must have the wrong house." We both know that's not true. For starters, there are no other houses anywhere near where I live.

I close the door in his face and watch him retrace his steps down the hill. He pauses for a moment until he sees me, standing in the window, watching him through the binoculars. For a time he fades from view, concealed by the six matching post oak trees that arch from either side of my driveway and meet in the middle like a dappled green porte cochere. When he emerges on the other side of the trees he vaults over the gate, swinging his body in one continuous movement as though he's an Olympic gymnast. I watch as he crosses the road and disappears down the access road of the freeway like he's never been to my house and knows nothing about me or my husband, Philip.

The burly guy was the messenger, but the real question is: Who's brazen enough to send such a malevolent message? It's not the first. Especially if I count the men in suits, driving a four-door sedan, who stop at the foot of our hill and empty the contents of our garbage can into their trunk. But even that wasn't the first time.

I steady my binoculars and focus on the Exxon station across the street, searching for signs of the stranger who knocked on our door. Until now, I didn't have a possible face to go with the voices I heard outside my bedroom window or the shadows that moved back and forth in the gap between the bottom of the bedroom door and the floor. Perhaps he was the one who'd brushed up against the other side of the door when Philip was passed out in bed beside me. A result of too much cocaine and alcohol.

The sickly little girl I used to be, the one with asthma who slept on four and sometimes five pillows just to breathe, never could have imagined she would one day pull a shotgun from a secret compartment next to her bed. Or that she would walk naked and barefoot to the door and chamber a round—an unmistakable sound to anyone who isn't deaf—and fling open the door in time to see three grown men, tripping over one another as they stumbled down the stairs and out the dungeon door. Men in dark slacks who'd overridden our alarm system, not punks in blue jeans who'd busted open a window to steal a stereo. But even that wasn't the first time, or the second, or the third. And I can't forget the people who break into Philip's lab, or rifle through the papers on my desk upstairs, or leave my sheer black thigh-highs in the same drawer as my belts. Something I would never do.

I sink into the sofa in front of the bedroom window and scan the driveway and the bottom of our hill at the intersection where Judson Road crosses over the freeway. There's an endless line of traffic on IH-35, the north-south interstate that stretches from the Mexican border, past my house in San Antonio, Texas, up through the American heartland to Duluth, Minnesota. Like every other day, it's bustling with cars and midsize trucks and eighteen-wheelers. Busy people going about their day, oblivious to the sinister stranger who knocked on my door. People who are clueless about the respected Dr. Jekyll and the haunted Mr. Hyde who's crept into my bed. The same man who's my husband and, until three years ago when the cocaine and alcohol took over, made me feel safe and loved.

Perhaps I'm reading more into the burly guy's message than

I should. Maybe he'd been playing a prank, or maybe he was one of the curiosity seekers who wanted to say they'd been to the infamous "Spy House on the Hill."

Like the old man and his granddaughter who let carrier pigeons go in our driveway, or the notorious "motorcycle club" who brought a professional photographer with his panorama camera to take their Christmas card photo in the same place. Twenty members—one with a small silver skull braided into his beard—wearing matching vests had roared up our hill and parked their bikes side-by-side as the sun set and the city lights shimmered behind them, and their motorcycle babes stood off to the side and watched.

I've lived here for ten years, behind a locked gate on the highest hill in town. Even before we bought the abandoned "Spy House on the Hill," as it's known, it was a place wrapped in mystery and fabled stories. It's one of those houses people talk about and wonder who lives here. If the stories about it are true. An intriguing dwelling shrouded in history and hearsay. A three-story, 6,400-square-foot Art Deco treasure that safeguards and yet screams of scandalous secrets hidden inside.

This afternoon, before the burly guy knocked on my door, I'd been sitting here trying to get a handle on how my life had gotten so far off track. It's difficult to comprehend that I'm at the center of another one of the house's shocking secrets. One that began with my husband, Jon Philip Ray, a brilliant and prominent entrepreneur admired by everyone, a man I've loved and worshipped most of my adult life—since we first started seeing one another when I was twenty-one and he was thirty-three. But now we're keeping a secret so dark, it feels as though we've descended into quicksand, and the only way out has collapsed into a sinkhole behind us.

The stranger at my door has confirmed what I've known

since childhood: Neither my parents, my husband, a locked gate, the sign at the foot of the hill, nor an alarm system can protect me. I'm the only one I can count on to be here for myself, and I live in a world where I'm afraid to show my vulnerabilities for fear they will rob me of the strength I need to survive. But I don't allow myself to dwell on these things or I'll stay rooted in fear and wind up powerless like Mother.

I've never understood why Mother likes being the victim. I didn't get that gene or maybe I've edited it out of my DNA. As far back as I can remember, even before we role-reversed, I was the grownup in our relationship: ready, if necessary, to respond to her emotional meltdowns. Even as a young child, I knew how to hang on and survive in a crisis.

"You think I'm crazy, don't you?" she's fond of saying. Sometimes she'll quote from *My Fair Lady* and drop the "H" from Henry and Higgins as Eliza Dolittle does. "You think I should be in the looney bin! Well, just you wait 'enry 'iggins. Just you wait!"

When there are no further signs of the burly guy, or of "Guido and Little Louie," the names Philip and I've given the guys who steal our garbage and the ones who break into our home, I return the binoculars to the windowsill. Maybe instead of sitting here, thinking about them, I should be asking myself how Philip got so far off course. He's the last person anyone would suspect of making drugs. Cocaine to be exact.

Or maybe instead of wondering how Philip lost his way, I should be asking myself why I haven't asked him to stop what he's doing. Why I haven't said, "Shut down the lab, or I'm leaving you."

CHAPTER TWO

Three Years Ago

I'M RESTORING THE LEGENDARY SPY HOUSE ON THE HILL one room at a time. I've taught myself how to patch plaster walls and how to remove bad patch jobs down to the original chicken wire, and I know the house down to its bare wood studs. I'm turning an ugly duckling into a swan and making it my own. It's detailed and tedious, but this house has my heart. Common sense tells me inanimate objects don't have feelings, but sometimes I imagine this house loves me as much as I love it.

This morning I'm working on the original crown molding where the wall meets the ceiling. When I stop to clean the plaster from the small trowel in my hand, I'm reminded of the first day Philip and I walked through the front door. Our friend, a real estate investor who owned it before us, had warned us the house needed a lot of work.

"It's been abandoned for years and in shabby condition," he said. "It's the place where kids go to party and vagrants spend the night. My wife doesn't want anything to do with it. The house scares her."

That first day, it was obvious this wasn't an ordinary house. The majestic bedroom overlooked the city and the ornate Art

Deco his and hers dressing rooms exuded round-the-clock whiffs of glamour and mystery that wafted their way through most of the house. The dirty wall-to-wall gold carpeting was strewn with empty beer cans, and the walls were scrawled with graffiti, but I could see past the cosmetic blemishes to the bone structure of the house. Even in its initial state of disrepair, it was breathtaking. I didn't need to go any further. I loved this house, and I could see us being happy here.

I remember the way Philip took my hand. How we'd stood spellbound as the city unfolded at our feet. Philip, who'd lived in a one-room tin shack with a dirt floor as a boy, and me, the little girl who'd lived in a small square house with an erratic and emotionally unstable mother.

"You're going to have to carry me out of here in a pine box," I'd told him. We'd looked at one another and, without saying another word, we knew we were home. A brand-new feeling washed over me that day: a sense of permanence and belonging, and I knew our adventurous, adrenaline-filled life would have roots and room to grow.

As I finish cleaning the trowel in my hand, I'm startled to see a man outside on our veranda. He's waving at me through the picture window.

"Mitch Krueger suggested I stop by and tell you what I know about the house," I can hear him say.

I don't recognize him, but if our friend, Mitch, the one we bought the house from, suggested he should stop by, then that's good enough for me.

The man on the veranda is old enough to be my grandfather, and once he takes off his cowboy hat, I can see the contrast between his tanned face and the top of his pale, smooth bald head. When I open the door, he extends his hand. It has the rough texture of a working man's hand.

"Do you know how the Spy House got its name?" he asks.

"My husband and I've heard rumors that Nazi spies lived here, but we don't know if they're true."

"Oh, they're true all right. I was a young officer with the Bexar County Sheriff's posse when they arrested them. This was the perfect place for the Nazis to keep an eye on how America's war effort was escalating during World War II." He points to the wall-to-wall, floor-to-ceiling windows in the living room. "They spied on Randolph Air Force Base over there and kept track of the number of pilots they trained."

His story rings true because, on a clear day, I can read the names on the pilot's flight suits with the Celestron 8 telescope our friend, Rick, keeps in our living room. A fitting accent piece for the Spy House on the Hill.

"Have you discovered the secret room yet?"

The words "secret room" thrill me with the prospect of something eerie and exciting and reminds me of the Nancy Drew mysteries I devoured as a kid.

"No, but if I had to guess, I'd say it has something to do with the deadbolt locks upstairs."

"Well, what do you know! They're still there."

Without asking for permission, this man, who seems to know more about my house than I do, bounds up the stairs to the third floor. At the top of the landing, he pauses to catch his breath.

"I'm not as young as I used to be." In the wide hallway outside my office, he points to three closets next to one another. "The spies kept their communication room up here, but you have to know the precise place to push on the wall, or you'll never find it."

Inside, the closets look like any cedar-lined closets used to store sweaters and winter coats to protect them from moths. The retired sheriff makes sure I'm watching as he opens the closet on the left and then pushes on the coat hook in the center of the wall. As if by magic, the wall swings open to reveal an empty space.

I glance inside and back at him with wide eyes. "No way!" He wasn't kidding. There's a secret room in my house. My very own Nancy Drew mystery. It's easy to see the retired sheriff is happy he's the one who showed it to me.

"When we made the arrest, this room was filled with maps and radios and a telescope. The cabinets above the closet. Have you looked inside those yet? You'll need a ladder, but . . ."

Before he can finish his sentence, I've retrieved the ladder I've been using to paint the walls in my office. I climb the bottom two rungs and open the cabinet door on the wall above the secret room. The first thing I see is an old porcelain light fixture with a beaded metal chain hanging down. When I pull on the metal strand, the light comes on.

"Amazing! After all these years, the lightbulb's still good."

"What do you see?" he asks.

"It's bigger than a crawl space but not big enough to stand upright in, and it wraps around behind the other two closets. And there's an old hot plate plugged into the wall."

My mind is spinning with my new discoveries, but most of all, I'm astonished to be peering into history. The lights and the hot plate tell me the spies were prepared in case they needed to spend an extended time in hiding. With my next breath, my excitement dissolves into something sinister and evil.

"There's a Nazi swastika carved into the wall." I hesitate, then lightly trace the symbol with my finger. I imagine the crawl space and the secret room when it was full of telescopes and radios and Nazi officers. *Did they wear their uniforms when they were here, or on the off chance a stranger might stop by, per-*

haps they dressed like Americans to blend in with the locals? One thing is for sure. I will never think about my office and the closets upstairs in the same way again. If only this house could talk.

Before he leaves, the sheriff shows me more secrets my house has been keeping: the hidden wall safes downstairs. One is in my dressing room closet, and there's a matching one in Philip's dressing room closet as well. Like the secret room on the third floor, it's all about knowing the right place to push on the wall.

In the closed position, the cedar paneling on the safe's exterior fits neatly into place with the rest of the paneling around it. As though I'm performing a magic trick, I delight in sliding the paneling up to reveal the hidden safe and back down again to make it disappear. Now you see it, now you don't. I could have lived here forever and never discovered any of them.

Inside is an area tall enough to fit four or five books, standing upright, plus there are two dovetailed wooden drawers with brass pull rings. The workmanship is precise and beautiful, and I wonder what the Nazi spies kept hidden here. I'm almost giddy over my newfound covert compartments. Oh, the things I could safeguard there, and if need be—although I don't know why—Philip and I could hide in the secret room upstairs.

But the most intriguing thing I've discovered about this house is not the secret room or the wall safes. It's something most people will never experience or understand. This isn't a house where you close the door and live here. Instead, you put it on and wear it like you would your most intimate piece of clothing.

The house has seduced us. It's become a part of us, our moods, and the way we think. Living here is a way of life, and except for Philip's project in the dungeon, I love everything about it.

CHAPTER THREE

THE SPY HOUSE ON THE HILL BEGAN AS A SMALL one-story rock structure built in the early 1900s, twenty miles from downtown San Antonio. In the 1930s, it became the centerpiece for the larger three-story house constructed around it. Inside the walls of the old rock house, in the heart of the dungeon, is where Philip has set up an organic synthesis chemistry lab.

As I flip on the downstairs light, I'm reminded of why I call this place the dungeon. Beginning with the hollow sound my feet make on the wooden staircase, there's something down here that makes the hair on my arms stand at attention. The rest of the house is open and full of light, but down here, it's dark and dank. It's the place where scorpions thrive, and the back of my neck crawls with the feeling something terrible happened here, but for some reason, I don't think it's related to the Nazi spies.

The door to the lab is open, and Philip is taking the tare weight of a glass beaker. He looks happy and content, absorbed in his project, a self-taught organic synthesis chemist, making complex molecules that have never existed before and reducing them like a chef reduces a roux.

He sees me standing in the doorway. "Careful what you

touch." He doesn't have to say anything more because I know his rules about the lab are hard and firm. "Everything down here is poisonous."

Everything down here is poisonous. He reconfirms my feelings about the dungeon. It already has an unspoken "Danger Keep Out" sign, but now he's raised the stakes by working down here with caustic chemicals.

"Have you ever seen mercury?" he asks.

I shake my head *no* and move closer as he dons a pair of thick orange rubber gloves and opens a sealed airtight cylinder. He peels back the top. Inside is a round slab of mercury.

While I've been restoring the rest of the house, Philip has transformed the kitchen in the old rock farmhouse into a scientific laboratory. He's built a worktable next to the original chipped white porcelain sink and installed an overhead vent hood with a fan designed to take any toxic fumes outside. He's made sure the shower and the toilet in the old bathroom are in working order, he's purchased fire extinguishers and a new refrigerator, and he's made it clear that food and drink are not allowed inside.

"See how it's this dull grey on the outside? Watch what happens when I cut into it." The round piece of mercury cuts like butter, and inside it looks like polished sterling silver. "It won't take long before it oxidizes and turns grey like it has on the outside."

On the worktable in front of him are varying sizes of Pyrex glass beakers, Erlenmeyer flasks, and clear glass condensation coils that remind me of long pieces of fusilli pasta. There are glass separatory funnels that would be perfect for separating grease from homemade chicken stock, glass pipettes, thermometers, a Corning Ware magnetic stir plate, and a small torch he uses to make glass stir rods.

"Now watch what happens when I break the tiny piece I just cut."

He grins at me like a kid with a secret. His enthusiasm for science is contagious, and he makes learning—about everything—fun. He's like living with Mr. Wizard, and there's nothing better than seeing his eyes light up when he has a challenge. It wasn't long ago I thought I'd never see that look again, but then we didn't know a week without Valium could cause seizures. Valium is the little round pill he takes to shut down his brilliant mind long enough to let him sleep.

With the flat blade of his knife, he gently smashes the small piece of mercury, and like magic it turns into a dozen shiny silver balls the size of BBs that begin rolling across the table. With a gloved hand, he gathers them up and puts them in a special trash container.

"Mercury's deadly to touch or inhale. It's one of the reasons for the vent hood."

Nothing topples Philip Ray. He is a tower of strength and logic, but the morning I now think of as "the Valium incident," he'd marched back and forth across the top of our king-sized bed, unable to string a simple sentence together. We were thousands of miles away from home, and he'd forgotten to refill his prescription before we left. After a week without Valium, he'd started rocking back and forth. A doctor we didn't know checked him into a local psych ward. I watched through reinforced glass panes in a pair of locked double doors as he was led away in a white canvas straitjacket, his arms buckled behind his back. Then, as well as now, he won't discuss it. All I know is the experience has changed him.

Now, as I listen to him tell me about mercury, it occurs to me he would make a great teacher. Perhaps it's on his list of future careers. I hope he begins thinking about one of them soon. I've done everything I can to help him find the old Philip: the happy man he was before accidentally going cold turkey on Valium had rewired the way the synapses fire in his brain.

I don't like what he's doing down here in the lab, but if I'm honest with myself, I've played a part in this too. I've enabled him by staying silent because I've always trusted him to do what's in our best interest.

No . . . that's not the reason I've stayed silent. It's what he said to me in the early days of our relationship. *This is my train, and you're welcome to ride it. If at any time you don't like the destination, you're free to get off, but you won't find a better ride anywhere.*

His declaration has made an indelible tattoo on my brain. He might as well have stamped it there with a branding iron because ten years later, the same statement continues to take up a vast amount of real estate in my head. It's why I've always wanted what he wants. I'm driven by this low-grade fear that I might be asked to get off at the next stop.

Everything I do is because of, and for, him. Since the day we started seeing one another, I've wanted to be like no woman Jon Philip Ray has met or ever would meet. I wanted to be the one he couldn't live without. I've reinvented myself from the little girl with asthma who couldn't take PE or play outside to a woman who does almost anything he wants whether it's adventurous, dangerous, sexual, or illegal, but I've done more than that. I'm complicit in a drug lab.

CHAPTER FOUR

REGARDLESS OF WHAT I'M DOING, MY THOUGHTS ARE never far from what's happening in the dungeon. Philip didn't set out to build a drug lab, but after the Valium incident, he wanted time away from the business world and the rigors of starting another public company like Datapoint Corporation. Philip and his business partner conceptualized and developed the world's first desktop computer terminal, the Datapoint 3300, followed by the first smart personal computer, the Datapoint 2200. Wall Street predicted it would change the world, and it has.

"I want a one-man project that doesn't involve writing business plans and raising money for risky startups, or dealing with temperamental geniuses and anxious investors," he'd told me. Something that would be more challenging than the gold and silver lost-wax castings we made from the scorpions and spiders and leaves we found in the backyard. A hobby that was good for killing time until he got himself on track, again.

The idea to make cocaine had come from an unlikely source: a flawless diamond we saw at the Smithsonian Institution's Museum of Natural History. The stunning stone wasn't a synthetic imposter like the ones advertised on late-night TV for "three easy payments of thirty-nine, ninety-nine." The dazzling stone was a *real* diamond, made by General Electric, and it had resurrected Philip's lifelong interest in what he calls "increased value."

"This diamond began as something that had little or no value," he'd explained that day. "It's carbon, together with extreme amounts of heat and pressure, that's been transformed into something of greater value. Like when my brother turned a small block of wood into a model car and won a full-ride college scholarship."

He didn't bring it up, but I know the first microprocessor, known as the 8008 computer on a chip that he and his company, Datapoint, invented is another example of increased value. The chip began with silicon and oxygen and is now the future of medicine and motion pictures, hairdryers, and haute couture.

"I wonder if anyone's figured out how to make real emeralds?" he'd asked that day.

Emeralds are Philip's favorite stone, and I could see him heading up a technology-based effort to make real emeralds. It was a perfect fit. A suitable venture that could put the Valium incident in the rearview mirror.

I know my way around a library, especially the library at Trinity University where I graduated. It's the same library where I research places for us to dig for truncated quartz and amethyst crystals along with azurite and malachite in abandoned silver mines in New Mexico, Arizona, and Mexico and undiscovered Maya ruins in the jungles of the Yucatán. When I researched manmade emeralds, I discovered someone had already done it, but instead of being disappointed with my news, Philip had handed me the weekly news magazine he'd been reading. The cover story was about cocaine.

The expensive white powder is no longer just for Hollywood and the jet set. Mom and Pop America are risking freedom, finances, jobs, and even death for another snort of the elusive cocaine high.

"Cocaine's another example of increased value," he'd said. "It begins as a leaf and turns into something people are willing to risk everything to possess. I wonder if anyone's figured out how to make it? Surely, they have."

For Philip, it had been nothing more than a benign brain-teaser. He was a man with a question in search of an answer. It's his specialty, and an unanswered question is more than he can bear.

That same afternoon, he'd accompanied me back to the university's library where, at his direction, I searched for information on the chemical structure of cocaine—$C_{17}H_{21}NO_4$. He wasn't interested in any of the synthetic "go fast" substances like speed. The magazine article said any backwoods idiot could make speed in their bathtub.

At the library, I found an 1894 reference to Dr. Richard Willstätter, a Nobel Prize-winning German chemist and an expert on alkaloids—naturally occurring substances like morphine, opium, caffeine, nicotine, and cocaine. Willstätter's doctoral thesis was on the compounds that make up cocaine, but his paper was in German. The only other related papers I found were in Russian. None were in English.

Over the next few months, Philip and I had piled up in bed with German and Russian-English dictionaries and the papers from the library while our dog, Phydaux, lay at the end of the bed and slept. The translation process was slow and tedious, but I loved it. We were together, deciphering a mystery. It was the first fun we'd had in almost a year, since before he'd accidentally stopped taking Valium. He had something that challenged and engaged him, and it was all that mattered to me.

Since neither one of us could understand Russian or pronounce the Russian alphabet, we developed nicknames for the letters that didn't look like they were a part of any language.

"Capital *B*, capital *O*, musical note, small *b*, *l*," Philip would call out.

In the Russian-English dictionary, I would find the capital *B* and run my finger down the page until I located the capital *O*, followed by the musical note and the other two letters. Воды.

"Water," I said. "It means water."

Sometimes we'd lean back and laugh at the preposterous nature of what we were doing, but all I cared about were the glimpses I was getting of the old Philip. The one with the twinkle in his eye and the magical spellbinding gift for explaining the most complex subject in simple understandable terms. Friends and business associates cluster around him like children during story time, and walk away thinking they understand how electricity works, the basics of physics, or something as complicated as string theory.

I would have sat there translating papers with him for the next six months if I thought it would have sparked his imagination and gotten him back on track. I was sure that at some point, he would move on to something more in keeping with his engineering and entrepreneurial background. This wasn't a man who would make drugs. I would have bet my life on that. Besides, neither one of us was interested in trying cocaine.

We were clueless about the drug's appeal or how our good friend and investment partner, a Hollywood concert promoter, fell prey to it and overdosed and died. And even if we'd wanted to try it, there were easier ways than attempting to pull an old Russian genie out of a bottle and make complicated compounds in a laboratory. By my way of thinking, what Philip was doing was the equivalent of giving Phydaux a Julia Child cookbook so he could make beef Wellington and Madeira sauce in our kitchen. I viewed what we were doing as busy work until Philip was ready to reenter the business world.

That last afternoon, when Philip spelled the final word, I remember it had a mirrored *k*, and a backward *n* with a smile over it. Осторожный.

"Caution," I'd said. "It means caution."

CHAPTER FIVE

WHEN PHILIP FIRST STARTED WORKING IN THE LAB, I would stop what I was doing and go downstairs every hour, stand in the doorway, and ask how things were going. I wanted to make sure he was all right. Since his first days in the lab nothing has changed, and I worry about him to the point it's difficult for me to concentrate on anything else. I'm driven by my need to check and recheck that he isn't sprawled out on the floor, overtaken by toxic fumes or poisoned by the chemicals in the shiny glass beakers.

To ease my fears—and maybe some of his own—Philip has set up an intercom between the lab and the main bedroom suite on the second floor so I can hear what's happening. In addition, I keep both doors to the dungeon open, the one from the kitchen and the door near the back bedroom, so I can hear if something goes wrong. But it doesn't make me any more comfortable with what he's doing downstairs. Everything about it is dangerous and shady, and that's not the man I married.

This time, as I make my way down the stairs to the lab, I'm hoping he'll tell me he's at a stopping point and we can spend some time together, but I'm not counting on it. The pages we translated, the ones he spent months reworking by himself, are now what he calls "the recipe," and they've turned into his own personal Rubik's Cube.

I believed our translation exercise had been a temporary stopgap until something worthy piqued his interest, but his one-man project has turned into an all-consuming undertaking I didn't foresee. I would never tell him this, but I'm dumbfounded he's gotten this far. By my way of thinking, based on our amateur Russian translations, making cocaine is a farfetched goal like building a time-travel machine. I keep hoping he'll tell me the task is impossible and he's decided to abandon it, but I also know giving up isn't in his nature.

"What's in the beaker?" I ask. I keep my voice light because every time I come downstairs, I don't want him to think I'm here to pressure him into stopping.

He rattles off a complicated chemical name, three numbers followed by a string of Latin words I've never heard. "Just think of what I'm doing as baking a cake except I have to make all the starting ingredients from scratch. The flour, the sugar, and the baking powder."

He's cautious and methodical, and he always sets a timer so he knows precisely when it's time for something to be filtered, or when he needs to shake the contents of a separatory funnel.

"I'm refining the recipe until each ingredient of the starting material is pure before I put them all together in 'the mixing bowl.'"

Unlike the restoration work I'm doing on the house, I can't tell whether he's making any progress, so the concept of actually making cocaine is vague and hazy at best. It's not a mechanical object like the laser machine he made with knobs and mirrors that projects patterns on the wall. At least that was something we could share with friends, but now that the house reeks of chemicals, we no longer invite people over.

Philip must be reading my mind because just as I'm about to tell him I'm having second thoughts about what he's doing, he says, "I know it seems like I'm down here all the time, but some guys play golf. Other guys play poker or run around. I make cocaine." His statement sounds absurd, but he says it so matter-of-factly. "At least you'll always know where I am."

The lab has become his mistress, and she demands all of his time while I stand by, hoping she doesn't kill him. I would rather the windup timer she's outfitted him with made a sultry sound that cooed, "Philip. I need you. It's time for you to come back to me." But instead, it makes a jolting *rat-a-tat-tat* noise like a tinny toy machine gun, a sound I've come to dread.

His mistress interrupts everything. Christmas Eve I made a roast, exactly the way he likes it, but he couldn't get away from a reduction process to come upstairs and eat with me.

"Just leave it," he'd said. "I'll slice off a few pieces later and make a sandwich."

Fa-la-la-la-la . . . la-la-la-la. I might as well be living here by myself because if we can't eat a meal together, I don't foresee us doing something simple like going to dinner or the movies, much less going on one of our adrenaline-pumping adventure trips.

Since the day we started seeing one another, our relationship has crackled with electricity, in and out of bed. When we weren't having sex, we were racing Porsches in Sports Car Club of America events or hacking our way through three-canopy jungles or digging for minerals and crystals. We were Indiana Jones before there was an Indiana Jones, but now we rarely leave the house.

I've stopped restoring the third floor because what's happening in the dungeon keeps me tethered to the intercom on the second floor: the part of the house where the kitchen, the dining and living area, and the main bedroom suite are located. Without researching our next adventure or working on the house, I have nothing constructive to occupy me other than waiting for something to go dreadfully wrong downstairs. For the fabric of our life together to come undone like a piece of exquisite silk that's been ripped apart.

"I've been thinking about getting a job," I tell him. "I need something to do other than working on the house."

Philip has never wanted me to have a job, and I don't want to be a "kept woman," as my grandmother used to say. Children aren't high on our priority list. I've already had a child—my mother—and Philip has two from his previous marriage he seldom sees. The women of my generation are breaking through glass ceilings, but other than working freelance on a Gulf Oil commercial and a few documentary films, I've chosen Philip over having a career. The feeling of being loved is stronger than any drug I can imagine.

"You know, if you have a job, we won't be free to travel whenever we want," he says. "We won't be able to go on our trips and our expeditions." It's not the first time he's said this to me. "Someday you'll look back and be glad you did all these things. No one has adventures like we do."

Part of me is tempted to say, "You mean like when our rental car broke down near the abandoned silver mine in the middle of nowhere? And before the sun went down and the temperature dropped to freezing, you stayed to fix the car while I ran for help —miles across the desert to the nearest backwater road. Before the rattlesnakes slithered out to soak up the remaining warmth of the rocks, and the bobcats and coyotes came out to hunt for rabbits. Or are we talking about something simple like waiting for a procedure to go wrong in the lab and the house blows up?"

For some time now, Philip and I've been moving toward opposite ends of the same spectrum. He's as obsessed with his scientific project as he would be with a new lover, while I sit by, helpless, like I'm freefalling toward the end of everything we've ever known. But each time I think about telling him how I feel, I stop myself. It's not that I can't access my feelings, because I can, and I'm not a pushover or a doormat, but sometimes it's easier when I keep my emotions sequestered on a shelf.

Since childhood I've been conditioned to pretend every-thing's okay, and if it isn't, I remain calm and stoic in case I need to take charge. Like when my father died on my thirteenth birthday and Mother retreated to her room with the shades pulled, or when Philip was released from the psych ward and sat on the edge of our bed for six months, silent and withdrawn like a mannequin in a darkened storeroom.

We've never talked about the fact that while he sat in the dark, I secretly ran his high-tech startup company. Decisions needed to be made, but instead of telling investors and em-ployees what happened, I told them he had a mysterious illness related to the removal of his spleen the year before. Philip may not admit it, but he depends on me, and I don't want to fail him.

I've begun to wonder, *At what point does his project downstairs become illegal?* What if there comes a time when he's crossed a line, when the substance he's working on becomes illegal, and because I know what he's doing, I will have crossed the line as well?

I imagine a headline in *The Wall Street Journal* that reads, "Inventor of Personal Computer and Wife Arrested for Making

Cocaine." But since he tells me he's still at the "flour and baking powder" stage, what concerns me most is whether the chemicals will blow us up in the middle of the night. *Boom!* The last of the salacious secrets about the storied Spy House on the Hill will have disappeared forever, and us along with them.

CHAPTER SIX

I DON'T NEED AN INTERCOM TO HEAR THE CRASH coming from downstairs. It's the sound of breaking glass, together with a loud thud, and in seconds I'm racing down the back stairs to the dungeon.

As usual, the door to the lab is open, and the first thing I see is Philip's black swivel chair. Overturned. The chair has come undone from the four-legged rolling wheels. Broken glass is scattered about the base of the chair and liquid is seeping into the thin, raggedy blue carpeting that's been there since the beginning of time.

Philip's cowboy boots, his underwear, jeans, and shirt are on the floor, but he's nowhere to be seen. It would be almost impossible to remove all his clothes and disappear in such a short amount of time. It's as though his flesh and bones have dissolved in the ten seconds it took me to sprint downstairs.

Scary, half-formed scenarios tear through my mind faster than I can process them, and I'm reminded of the Wicked Witch of the West after Dorothy doused her with water. The witch's body had grown smaller and smaller until she'd disappeared into the ground with nothing left but her clothes. "I'm melting!" she'd cried. "I'm melting." But I know that's preposterous.

I hear the faint sound of running water coming from the

small bathroom next to the lab. When I rush in and pull back the shower curtain, Philip's standing there, naked and grinning at me, as he scrubs the inside of his left thigh with a wire bristle brush.

"Oh!" My hand flies to my mouth to stifle the part of me that feels like I've stumbled upon the apocalypse, and I'm witnessing one of the walking dead. My first thought is that the grin is designed to keep me calm and make me believe everything is all right, but clearly things are not all right.

His leg looks like a piece of raw, bloody hamburger meat. I shudder and resist the urge to turn away in horror as Philip makes repeated downward motions to his leg with the wire bristles. Instead, I do what I've been conditioned to do since childhood: I pretend to be calm.

"What happened?"

"I swiveled one too many times, and the chair came undone from its post, but I'm okay."

With each stroke of the wire brush, he's debriding the flesh from his leg like he's scraping peeling paint off the side of an old house. Blood and bits of flesh are whirling together with the water from the shower and being washed down the drain.

I imagine his pain level must be off the charts, but he continues to smile at me like it's no big deal. I think about the deadly chemicals that have been absorbed into his bloodstream, and I want to cry out, but I don't. The horrendous thing I've been waiting for has happened and inside I'm dizzy and reeling. My heart feels like it's going to take flight out of my chest, but I need to stay calm and remain in control.

"I'm okay," he says again. "Would you run upstairs and bring me a clean towel and some hydrogen peroxide, please?"

Like the grin, I know the "please" is designed to show me he's not worried, and I shouldn't be either. Then again, maybe it's his way of keeping himself calm as well. This is not a minor cut or gash. The inside of his leg looks like roadkill. It's red and bloody like a freshly slaughtered animal.

In less than sixty seconds, I'm back with the towel and the hydrogen peroxide. Philip is still scrubbing his leg, hard, with the wire brush.

"Would you open the hydrogen peroxide and hand it to me, please?" His voice is low-key, as though he's doing a menial task like washing the dishes.

I hand him the opened bottle and watch, spellbound, as he pours the contents into the gaping wound. Even with the water running, I can hear the hydrogen peroxide bubble as it mixes with the ragged tissue on the inside of his leg. Now I can see all of the wound. It's oval-shaped, about six inches long and four inches wide, and it's deep like a crater on the surface of the moon. He uses the towel to dry himself off, careful not to touch that part of his leg, then wraps himself in the blue velour bathrobe and steps into the deck shoes I've brought.

Even with the vent hood and all his precautions, there are times when I'm upstairs and I catch a whiff of chemicals, but here, in the midst of the spill, the smell is biting on the back of my throat. I can feel it and taste it on my tongue, and I know the same chemicals are pumping through his bloodstream and his brain. *What if they kill him or at the very least, make him dangerously ill? If I can smell them sometimes, what are they doing to me?*

"One second, I was shaking the separatory funnel, and the next, the chair tipped over. As I went down, the long end of the glass funnel hit the edge of the counter and broke, and the contents spilled on my leg."

Philip reaches for a garbage bag and a box cutter on the counter and then dons the pair of thick orange rubber gloves. He stuffs his boots and his clothes in the garbage bag and then proceeds to cut away the wet section of carpeting and carefully lifts them into the bag. He uses a piece of cardboard to brush up the broken glass onto another piece of cardboard and then adds it to the bag. When he's done, he turns the chair back on its wheels and makes sure he's spun it down, so it doesn't topple over again.

"For now, there's nothing else I can do down here."

It's as though I'm on autopilot and my brain hasn't registered the horror of what I've seen. I can almost imagine we've conducted a fire drill in some parallel universe so that on the day of a real catastrophe, we'll know how to respond with speed and efficiency. But if this were a fire drill, he wouldn't have a football-shaped hollow on the inside of his leg.

I follow Philip upstairs to the living room and sit next to him on the black L-shaped sofa. His favorite place to sit is in the corner, facing the city, with his legs stretched out in front of him. Except for the dim, twenty-five-watt bulbs hidden every six feet along the recessed cove of the ceiling, the rest of the room is dark, but there's enough light for me to see his leg.

"The wound on your leg is bigger than I first thought." It's half an inch deeper than the rest of his thigh, and I'm trying not to lose it because I've learned freaking out never helps anything. "I think we should get you to an emergency room."

"They wouldn't do anything I haven't already done." He takes a deep drag from the cigarette he's lit. "I scrubbed my leg until the flesh stopped falling off. I got to it, almost immediately, and then poured hydrogen peroxide on it. I'll keep doing the same thing so it doesn't get infected, but for now I'll keep it exposed to the air."

Until the flesh stopped falling off . . . Those words, in that order, are difficult for me to think about. *Until the flesh stopped falling off.* I wonder if anyone else has ever used those words, in that order, in a sentence.

The wall behind us is curved in a serpentine fashion, and the other two sides of the room are floor-to-ceiling, wall-to-wall windows that overlook the city. It's dark outside, and the moon is full. We sit in silence and stare at the city lights as they sparkle and stretch before us to the edge of the horizon. I watch the lights on a commercial airliner as it makes the final landing approach to the San Antonio International Airport across town.

"Besides . . . they're going to ask how I did this. What I spilled on my leg. Technically it's nothing illegal, but it's complicated."

It's more than what's happening downstairs that's complicated. It's how it's begun to affect our lives. Like what happened to Philip with the Valium, his project in the dungeon is one more thing I can't tell anyone. One more thing that makes me feel isolated and alone and reconfirms that it's never safe for me to relax.

The words to describe what I want to say are lodged in the back of my throat like a jagged piece of lumber stuck in a sawmill. Once again, I'm pretending life is fine and normal when it's not. I've cut off my highs and lows, and I'm living somewhere in the middle. It's a behavior that's a part of me like having blue eyes and auburn hair.

Outside on the freeway, there are never-ending rows of glittering red taillights, together with pairs of white headlights traveling in the opposite direction. It's almost hypnotic the way the first row of lights disappear over the crest of the horizon while others seamlessly take their place. Where are they all going this time of night? I imagine some are couples coming back from a party or the movies. People who would be shocked if they knew what was happening in the fabled Spy House on the Hill.

Tens of thousands of people pass by here every day, and at

one time or another, most of them have wondered who lives here. I've met strangers on airplanes to Albuquerque and Atlanta and on the beaches in Barbados and the Bahamas who've heard stories about my home. And yet, this infamous house, on one of the highest hills in Texas, is the perfect place to do most anything in plain sight without being seen.

If I told the people on the freeway that my house has a personality as strong and well-defined as any person I've ever known, they would think I'm crazy, but I'm not. The walls know what's happening here, and they're not surprised. The house has welcomed us and seduced us. It's made us feel removed from the rest of the world like we're living in our own country. But this world, the one on top of the hill at Judson Road and IH-35, rotates on another axis.

Over my shoulder, I see the lights from a military jet coming in for a landing at the nearby Air Force base. I think of the hidden rooms on the third floor where the Nazis were arrested for spying on the same military base. What if, like the previous residents, the house has given us free rein to venture down the wrong paths? Like the spies and the spirits in the dungeon, maybe we're part of an unspoken club that has secrets to keep. And like the residents who came before us, I fear our secrets will be our great undoing.

CHAPTER SEVEN

IT WASN'T THAT LONG AGO THAT PHILIP AND I REVELED in spending all of our time together. We were crazy about one another, joined at the hip. The Spy House on the Hill holds the blueprint for most of my adult life, and when I think back to a specific time or event, more than likely, it happened here in this house. Until now, they've all been happy memories.

The distance from the front door, down to the gate and back, five times, is a mile. I know this because Philip measured it when we used to walk it together. This afternoon, as I walk down the driveway alone, I think about all the times I've trimmed the bushes on either side of the drive and shaped the ivy on the low wall around the oversized car park, the part of the driveway that's topped with brick pyramids. At night, when the city lights come alive, the light bulbs inside the pyramids look like diamonds suspended from a sparkling piece of jewelry.

The car park on the top of the hill has been the launching pad for countless firework displays on the Fourth of July and New Year's Eve. With friends, we would chip in and buy boxes and boxes of wholesale fireworks. Strangers would pull up at the bottom of our hill and line both sides of Judson Road and the Sam's Club parking lot across the street. They would spread blankets on the hood of their cars and lean back against their front windshields as red chrysanthemums, yellow peonies, and bright white waterfalls rained down from the sky and the Rolling Stones' "Sympathy for the Devil" or Wagner's "Ride of the Valkyries" played from big Bose speakers on the veranda.

In preparation for the festivities, I would spend days cooking and getting ready, sometimes making tortellini from scratch. There's something soothing about the repetitive nature of making pasta. Running the dough through the pasta machine, again and again, hand cranking it until the pasta becomes thinner and thinner, then cutting it into three-inch squares and filling and folding each one into little shapes the Italians call "bishop's hats." While real Catholic bishop's hats are lined with silk and trimmed in gold, mine were filled with prosciutto, veal, and spinach and trimmed in butter and fresh grated Parmesan. Comfort food, Italian style. Other times I made pinto beans that took two days for the beer, brown sugar, and bourbon to meld until it was just right, while the guys made a spicy rub for the brisket they smoked outside.

Then there were movie nights when I made paella in a large blue-and-white enameled pan, or I put freshly cooked shrimp and raw oysters on ice in giant galvanized metal tubs and made large buckets of buttered popcorn. Everyone would curl up on the big L-shaped sofa, or the floor in front of it, while we screened 16 mm classic films like the 1955 French crime thriller *Rififi* and Michelangelo Antonioni's *Blow-Up*. Other times we would invite magicians to dazzle and mystify us with their talent. Our house was filled with friends and the joy of discovery. I never imagined life could be that happy and wonderful.

Now those days are behind us, and the inside of Philip's thigh continues to make me cringe. It's been months since the caustic chemicals ate away at his flesh, but his leg still looks like a piece of raw meat with a scattering of thick crusty scabs in the middle that look like overcooked burgers. The gory crater serves as a constant reminder that far worse things could happen, and every day, all day, I'm on guard, waiting for the proverbial "other shoe" to drop.

At this point, I can't imagine what it might be, but my little voice tells me it won't be anything good. Philip looks at everything in terms of risk and reward, and after ten years of marriage I understand where he's coming from, but there are no rewards for having a drug lab.

I'm afraid everything we hold dear will disappear in a blink! Not material possessions, but the things that matter most like health and love and life itself. I can't bring myself to tell him how I feel because then I'd have to confront the real basis of my fears. He brought it up only the one time, but I can never forget I'm on Philip's train. And if I tell him I don't approve of the lab, I run the risk of discovering my needs may not matter to him. I'm not ready to live with that.

"I'm very careful," Philip has assured me. "What happened with the chair and the separatory funnel was a fluke."

Despite his reassurances, it's difficult for me to concentrate on anything other than what's happening in the dungeon. No matter what I'm doing, I wind up creeping down the back staircase, just far enough to be able to see him through the open door to the lab. I'm compelled to go there—to make sure he's all right. And each time I find him happy and content, absorbed in what he's doing. But me? It's like I'm walking along the sharp edge of a knife blade. Waiting and wondering if, and when, the knife will slip and something worse will happen.

From the beginning of our relationship, I've known Philip becomes fixated on his projects. It's one of the things I love most about him. I like watching the meticulous, laser-focused way he has of working on something. He makes everything he does look easy, but I know it's not, which is something else I find attractive about him. But now, I wonder how I could have been so naive, especially when I've watched him tackle other complicated projects he knew nothing about because he stays with everything he tries until he's mastered it.

Like the wrecked and mangled RSK Porsche Spyder he bought. He restored the body and the engine and turned it into a winning race car. Sometimes I wish he was a butcher, a baker, a candlestick maker, or that I could turn back the clock on our fairytale life to when we traveled and explored for treasure. Those were things that brought us together, but like Philip, they've all vanished down a separatory funnel in the dungeon.

The nature of our lifestyle and what's happening downstairs makes it difficult for me to make friends, much less share anything about my life. I imagine those introductory get-to-know-you conversations with a new girlfriend over lunch.

"And what do you do?" she might ask. "And your husband, what does he do?"

"Oh, my husband makes cocaine. And me? I'm waiting for the time when it destroys us both."

I don't fit in. Most of the women I meet have children, but I have no parent-teacher meetings, soccer games, or college application essays to compare notes on, and they can't relate to the things I *can* talk about. And if I tell them about racing cars or our explorations in the jungles, they look at me as though I'm a freak of nature, like the two-headed lizard I saw in the Yucatán.

—•—

CHAPTER EIGHT

A FRIEND OF OURS IS A DOCTOR WITH ACCESS TO A gas-liquid chromatograph. The same machine law enforcement uses to test blood, urine, and hair samples for the presence of drugs and alcohol. He's called with the results of the substance Philip made in the lab.

Philip holds the receiver away from his ear so I can hear the other end of the conversation.

"What you sent me was 100 percent, pharmaceutical-grade cocaine. Doctors don't even have access to this stuff. Where'd you get it?"

"You're sure?" Philip asks.

"Of course, I'm sure! Where'd you get it?"

Philip sidesteps the question. "Thanks. I owe you one."

He's as excited as a kid on Christmas morning who got what he wanted from Santa. Against all odds, he's become a self-taught, organic synthesis chemist who's learned his efforts have been successful. He's made real cocaine from scratch.

I realize it's an incredible feat, but instead of being excited for him, somewhere in the not-too-distant future, I hear the sound of the other shoe.

I've set my own personal desires and career opportunities aside. The ones that use my journalism and film degree. I've done whatever it took to encourage and support him until he got himself back on track again. Before the spill on his leg, I considered his project downstairs as somewhat of a benign stepping-stone in that direction, but now I want him to shut down the lab. I want him to remove every glass pipette and stir rod. Every sinister canister of Mallinckrodt chemicals and clean it out as though it never existed. But I'm careful to edit my thoughts and present my feelings in a softer way.

"Congratulations," I manage to say. "Now that you've done it, do you think it's time for you to move on from the lab?"

"No. Now I want to see if there's a way to make cocaine from the skin of tomatoes, potatoes, and eggplant."

Even as he's telling me this, the words *cocaine* and *vegetable skin* in the same sentence sound absurd. Without hearing more, I want to say *no*, but once again, the words are lodged in the back of my throat.

Emotional conversations don't play well with Philip; he responds to calm and logic. I'm fighting to keep my composure, but I want to scream, *No! You can't do that!* I want to post my feelings on the big billboard across the freeway so he can see them every day, but instead I say, "What do vegetable skins have to do with cocaine?"

"They all contain hyoscyamine. One of the starting ingredients for cocaine. It's a long shot, but I'm going to look into it."

The anxious silence in my throat has now turned into a frightened thump in the middle of my gut. This is the project that will not die! Like the first "recipe," this means he'll start over with months of research and trial and error before he knows if it's even feasible. The idea is terrifying on so many levels, but I can't bring myself to come on strong and ask him to stop.

Philip is still talking about hyoscyamine, but I've tuned him out.

I've always thought of myself as a strong, gutsy woman, but I'm not. I'm a chicken heart. I've sold my voice in exchange for not feeling abandoned like when my father died, and I traded places with Mother and my childhood disappeared.

Philip says I'm the lowest-maintenance woman he's ever met. I used to interpret that as a good thing. I never complain. I'm not afraid of anything, and I do almost anything he asks, but now it's clear to me that I've overcompensated. In the process of being the perfect wife, I've given huge pieces of myself away.

Much of my self-worth comes from being with this man, but the hardest thing for me to come to terms with is that I've chosen his well-being over mine, because who would I be without him?

CHAPTER NINE

WHILE I'VE GIVEN UP RESTORING THE REST OF THE house and anything related to a journalism or film career, I've begun experimenting with black and white 35mm film, taking photographs of different objects in natural and artificial light. This morning I've arranged a basket of fresh button mushrooms on the butcher block in the kitchen, and I've set my camera on a tripod. Here I can hone my photography skills, and at the same time, if something goes wrong downstairs, I'm just a few feet away.

"Hey there." It's Philip. He's come upstairs and he's standing in the kitchen, holding a cigarette. "I've solved my smoking problem."

I watch as he brings the cigarette to his lips and inhales, but when he exhales, there's no smoke or vapor of any kind.

"I smoke because I'm addicted to the nicotine in tobacco. Cigarettes are nothing more than a drug delivery system to administer nicotine, but I don't want all the deadly chemicals and the two thousand byproducts of burning. Those are the things that kill you or give you cancer, not the nicotine."

He hands me the cigarette in his hand, but when I look closer, it's not a traditional cigarette. It's a small metal tube, the exact length and diameter of a cigarette, and he's covered the outside with white contact paper. On one end, he's wrapped it with a small bit of brown contact paper to make it look like the filtered end of a Winston or a Marlboro.

"There's nothing but nicotine inside, and I don't need to light it. I just inhale."

I turn it around and hold it up to the light and then take a sniff. The smell is sharp and abrasive. "How does it work?"

"Inside there's a microscopic amount of liquid nicotine on a piece of filter paper I've shaped to create a Venturi effect."

He leans against the kitchen counter and takes out a black Flair pen and a notecard from his shirt pocket and begins drawing an hourglass shape. He's making his explanation as simple as possible, but he's talking about fluid dynamics, the Italian scientist Giovanni Venturi, and Swiss mathematician Daniel Bernoulli. Principles and people I'm not familiar with, but they're all crucial to the design.

"You don't have to light it," he says again. "A smoker just breathes in the nicotine, and they get their fix. It's a smokeless cigarette."

Nothing Philip does surprises me, and if he says it works, I believe him. I put the metal tube up to my lips and inhale a small amount of air like I would if I were smoking a traditional cigarette. I can feel the nicotine on the back of my throat, and in a few seconds I get a little buzz.

"How long have you been working on this?"

"Two days."

"And how long have you been using it?"

"The same."

"Have you had a real cigarette?"

He shakes his head and smiles. "Not for two days."

Philip smokes a pack of cigarettes a day, and I'm surprised

the nicotine in this small metal tube has satisfied his cravings. "Do you have any desire to smoke?"

"No."

Other than an occasional cigarette with a glass of wine, I don't smoke, but the concept of a smokeless cigarette strikes me as nothing short of genius. And the best thing is it's legal. Please let this be the worthy venture I've been hoping for and the end of the project in the dungeon.

I'm a researcher at heart, and just as I've done with our adventure trips and the project in the dungeon, I'm at Trinity University's library, searching for credible data on nicotine and smoking, and this time, Philip is with me. Smoking is a hot-button issue at the moment, and almost every newspaper and periodical in the world has published numerous articles about the smoking controversy.

Nonsmokers say smoking is offensive and dangerous to their health, and they want it outlawed. At the same time, smokers are fighting for their right to smoke wherever they please, danger be damned.

Philip is on to something, and I'll do anything I can to make sure he stops making cocaine. I've copied the most concise and informative papers I've found about cigarettes and handed them to him.

"With all the health issues and the growing ban on smoking, a smokeless cigarette could change everything."

"Yes, but there's gotta' be a catch," he replies. "If this is such a great idea, why haven't the tobacco companies already done something like this?"

It's time for me to drill down and look for who, other than the tobacco companies, has something to gain or lose from a ban on cigarettes. It's not long before I find a reference to the "Big Six," the six largest tobacco companies that manufacture and market most of the world's cigarettes.

In a few minutes, another reference catches my eye: "The tobacco companies are selling a legal drug—more addicting than heroin—and it's killing their customers."

I read it aloud and ask, "How can the tobacco companies get away with this? Nicotine's an alkaloid and an addicting drug. Why isn't it classified as an illegal drug like heroin, cocaine, and morphine? Why is it the only alkaloid not controlled by the FDA, the Food and Drug Administration?"

While Philip studies the pages I've brought him, I find another article that outlines the relationship between the Big Six and the federal government. Specifically, the ATF—the Bureau of Alcohol, Tobacco, and Firearms.

"I think I found our money trail." Once again, I begin reading aloud.

> While the Big Six captures a yearly, multibillion-dollar worldwide monopoly on cigarettes, the ATF makes billions from the tax on cigarettes, the federal government's second-largest revenue source. The government's primary revenue source comes from the taxes on personal and corporate income.

"That's why the FDA hasn't classified cigarettes as an addicting drug," I say. "The government's making too much money! The Feds and the tobacco companies are in bed together!"

An hour goes by before I find another piece of the puzzle. "Listen to this! The way the government classifies tobacco products determines how they tax them. Your smokeless cigarette may not meet the government's legal definition of a cigarette: a tube-shaped tobacco product that is made of finely cut, cured tobacco leaves wrapped in nontobacco paper."

Philip scans the latest paper I've handed him. "We need an expert legal opinion on this, but if this is true . . ." He looks at the metal tube in his hand. "That would mean the ATF wouldn't be able to tax this like a cigarette. If this made it to the marketplace, think of all the revenue the federal government would lose out on."

"The Big Six wouldn't like it, either. If they sold fewer cigarettes—because of your smokeless cigarette—they'd lose billions."

"There's a legal loophole here big enough to hold all the tobacco farms in Virginia."

The university librarian has seen Philip inhaling from his smokeless cigarette, and she's walking toward our table. "I'm sorry, sir, but the library is a no smoking area."

Philip smiles at her. He's always gracious to everyone. "Thank you. I understand, but this isn't a regular cigarette."

The librarian looks puzzled and then brightens up and says, "Oh, I get it. You've got a pacifier to help you quit. A toy cigarette."

"Actually, there's nicotine in here. I'm inhaling it, but I don't need to light it."

"I've never heard of such a thing! My husband needs one of those! Where did you buy it?"

"It's not for sale. It's a prototype," he explains.

"Well, when it is for sale, I'll be the first person to buy one. Cigarettes are such nasty things, and I've told my husband if he wants to smoke, he has to go outside."

As the librarian turns to leave, I look at Philip and keep my voice low. "There are millions of other people just like her."

"Yes, but it's not that simple. The Feds and the Big Six can't afford to let this succeed."

"But if it did . . ."

Neither one of us finish my sentence. The implications, both positive and negative, are almost too far-reaching to think about.

CHAPTER TEN

MY UNDERWEAR'S IN THE WRONG DRAWER, AND I would never leave a rugged, brown hiking boot paired with a black peau de soie high heel. My hand recoils from my boot like it's a poisonous snake. This isn't the first time I've suspected someone's been going through my things, and it's been happening in my office as well.

I close the drawer of my dressing room closet and run upstairs. The neat stack of books on my desk is not as I left them. Last night, before we went to sleep, I took extra care to place my research papers on nicotine and the Big Six *just so* on my desk. I'd arranged them in a way only I would know if they'd been moved.

The fake note I labeled "Important!" is no longer sticking out from between the pages of the book at the top of the stack. Instead, the note is on my desk next to the phone. The warning bell in my head, the one that's been going off since the men in suits, driving four-door sedans, stopped at the foot of our hill and stole our garbage, is getting louder. And I feel a wave of the same terrifying feeling I get when I open the door to the dungeon.

In the hallway outside my office, I double-check the closets with the deadbolt locks and the secret room. The ones where the Nazi spies were arrested. Just as I hoped, they're empty, but like the dungeon, the third floor now give me the creeps.

Downstairs in our bathroom, Philip has a towel wrapped around his waist, and he's beginning to shave. I stand next to him and stare at his reflection in the bathroom mirror.

"Someone's been in my things. I didn't want to say anything until I was sure." I tell him about the drawers in my closet and the papers upstairs on my desk.

He stops shaving. His razor is in midair. "Really." His response is more of a statement than a question. "I didn't want to alarm you, but someone's been in the lab and my dresser drawers are a mess."

"But they don't take anything."

"No. They don't. A couple of weeks ago I gave the hinges on the outside of the lab door a light coat of paint, then dried them with a heat gun and locked the door. Both of us were gone that day, but when I got back, there were screwdriver marks on the hinges. Someone had removed the screws and tried to get into the lab." He rinses his razor and lays it on the edge of the sink. "Before we went to sleep last night, I took a long hair from your hairbrush and taped it across the door frame and the closed door to the lab. This morning, the hair was broken, but the tape was still in place."

The hair trick sounds like something out of a detective novel, but I believe him. It's not what I wanted to hear.

CHAPTER ELEVEN

SOMETIMES YOU KNOW THE TRUTH AS WELL AS YOU know the color of the sky, and sometimes the truth can ambush you when you're vacuuming. Like a few weeks ago when a corner of the carpet got sucked into the vacuum cleaner and revealed a golf-ball-sized baggie of cocaine. I didn't stop to think about what I should do. My response had been instinctual.

I'd ripped open the plastic bag and flushed the contents down the toilet, all the while saying, "Shit! Shit! Shit!" Until that moment I believed, or maybe I wanted to believe, my husband was downstairs researching hyoscyamine, tomatoes, potatoes, and eggplant. He's a scientist. It's the kind of thing he would do.

But when I confronted him about the cocaine I found, he'd glossed over it and said, "I thought I told you. The vegetable peel theory didn't pan out. And because a real organic synthesis chemist would say my methods are sloppy, I've been tinkering with the original recipe, working on increasing the purity and yield. Besides, it's a good way to decompress while I think about the next steps for the smokeless cigarette."

Tinkering, my ass! Since our conversation, he's been openly pulling out a razor blade and a mirror with lines of cocaine drawn across the top.

"I want to see what all the fuss is about," he told me. "Why people go snow blind and give up all reason and common sense to possess it. Why they go to extreme lengths to smuggle it and kill for it. Sell it, use it, and die for it."

It was another one of those lines he'd delivered with a straight face as though he was on a scientific mission of discovery, and I fell for it . . . or maybe I wanted to fall for it.

In hindsight, I should have said, "For a smart man, that's a dumb idea! We've already lost a friend to cocaine, and now you're trying to figure out how he got hooked in the first place. That makes no sense!"

When I tried cocaine, it was like I'd stuck a wet finger in a light socket. In seconds, I felt like I'd swallowed copious cups of coffee, followed by several shots of Italian espresso, and then raced, nonstop, to the top of the Empire State Building. I thought my heart would explode, but Philip? He loves the feeling he gets from cocaine, and now it's apparent he's doing more than tinkering. He's making his own personal stash, and all my brightly colored balloons full of hope, the ones where I believed he would get himself back on track, have burst in my face.

Hiding cocaine under the rug . . . that's something addicts do. If my husband is on his way to becoming a drug addict, then we're definitely on different trains. I'd almost prefer he was sleeping with another woman because hiding a secret supply of cocaine terrifies me even more.

The man I would do anything for is no longer acting in his best interest or mine. The blanket of trust I've held out for him has unraveled, and I've gone from being Pollyanna to being just plain stupid, and I have no one to talk to about it except Philip. Everyone we know admires him and whether they meant to or not, a conversation with them could close the loop, plus they might think less of him.

This isn't like the time he ran out of Valium, and I didn't

want people to misunderstand what happened to him. That wasn't his fault. His doctors never cautioned him about what would happen if he suddenly stopped taking it. How many secrets do I have to keep and for how long? Until death do us part?

CHAPTER TWELVE

IT'S BEEN MONTHS SINCE THE BURLY GUY KNOCKED on my door and warned we needed a bodyguard. Since then, life has continued to spiral downward in the wrong direction, and I'm worried about more than Philip working in the lab.

I would never have imagined secrets could be so heavy, or that I could never put them down. Like background noise in a busy restaurant, Philip's secret project in the dungeon is always competing for my thoughts. I'm exhausted and weary of living this way, but the only thing I have power over is myself and even that's sometimes difficult to master. For now, the best thing I can do is help him get the smokeless cigarette off the ground and, like the Valium incident, put the cocaine lab in the rearview mirror.

The smokeless cigarette needs a brand name, and I've made a list of words that might work, but none of them are right. This morning I pulled out a thesaurus that belonged to my father. Tucked away inside is a perfectly pressed maple leaf that's as least as old as I am. I wonder what made him save this particular leaf. Did it mark an event in his life? Was there a reason he put it between these two pages, or did he place it there at random? I know less about my father than I do about nicotine. Sad but true.

Many of the pages in his thesaurus are filled with words and notations he made in the margins with the mechanical pencil he always used. I study each word, looking for clues, but nothing jumps out at me. I'm not sure what I hope to find. Perhaps an insight into the man who kept me at arms-length. I don't remember much about him except he was overly strict, and I never seemed to please him. Perhaps that's another reason I'm reticent about speaking up to Philip. I don't want to disappoint the only other male figure in my life who, like my father, could abandon me. The thought strikes me as profound, and if I were sitting on a therapist's couch, I would say I've had an emotional breakthrough. But what do I do with it?

I scan the pages of the thesaurus until I zero in on the word *favor*, and a tagline jumps out at me: "Do yourself a favor and do those around you a favor by not smoking traditional cigarettes." In another minute, I coin the terms *vape* and *vaping*. Since users of FAVOR smokeless cigarettes are inhaling vapor, not smoke, I decide they're vaping instead of smoking. Both of them are terms no one has ever used before.

One month has folded into the next, and the brand name FAVOR and my tagline have appealed to everyone who's heard them. The attorneys have filed a trademark application for the name, and I've incorporated them into the business plan Philip and I are writing.

Philip has filed patent applications in the United States and numerous other countries, and he's put together a group of people to handmake hundreds of prototypes for ongoing medical and focus group studies. He has teams of attorneys, and he's using his money to pay for much of it. I think of it as "his money" because I'm clueless about our finances, and we've never shared a bank account.

This afternoon an investor is sitting on the black sofa in our living room. He doesn't smoke, but he's been holding a FAVOR smokeless cigarette and vaping away like crazy.

"It's brilliant Phil," he says. "But they won't let you get away with it, but if you do . . ."

We hear this every day, especially from our attorneys, but it doesn't prevent a potential investor from writing a check. Investors translate risk into something sexy, and everyone wants to be involved in a sexy deal because the upside is we could all become zillionaires.

The smokeless cigarette is on a fast track, but what if we've awakened a den of multibillion-dollar sleeping bears? The ATF and the Big Six. With all the patent filings and medical studies, the bears must know what we're doing. But the real question is: What will they do about it? And since Philip is continuing to work in the lab, my instincts tell me the Drug Enforcement Agency (DEA) could also be sniffing around. Bears are dangerous, and I don't think any of them will settle for foraging around in our closets.

—•—

CHAPTER THIRTEEN

PHILIP HAS STARTED WANTING MARATHON SEX SESSIONS that last through the night until well past dawn. I love sex but after hours and hours, nonstop, even sex becomes boring and feels like a chore. Maybe it's because I'm not doing cocaine, but I've come to dread what feels like endurance events. Then there are the mornings when daylight comes, and he wants more. Doesn't he know he'll never have an orgasm because he's had too much coke?

I want to scream, "Hello! Your big brain and your little brain are controlled by cocaine so there are no time limits on erections and orgasms!" But I stay silent because I know neither brain will hear me.

I just want to get it over with, grab some sleep, and get on with my day. I do my best to hasten it along, but instead, morning comes and we're still at it. There's something sad and sordid about looking out the window, watching the multitude of cars on the freeway. Busy people on their way to work while I'm still trapped in the den of iniquity.

It's eight o'clock in the morning, and Philip hasn't had an orgasm. "I need you to drive to the convenience store down the road and buy me a jug of wine," he says. He needs the wine to bring him down from all the cocaine he's snorted.

I don't like this Philip. I don't respect him, but I let him pressure me into going because if I don't, he will, and he's in no condition to drive or navigate the busy access road on the freeway.

While everyone else is purchasing a newspaper, their morning coffee, and a glazed donut, I get in line with my big glass gallon of cheap red wine. Who buys wine at this hour of the morning except for winos? I want the floor to open and swallow me whole.

In the last few months, I've copied numerous papers at the library about addiction and I've read countless books. With each one, I wanted to believe this would be the one that made him slap his forehead and say, "Of course! You're right! I'll stop!" It would be an 'I could have had a V8' moment', but that's not what happens. He tells me he has it under control, but standing in line with his gigantic jug of wine has flipped a switch somewhere inside me.

When I get home, I hand him his wine and the words come tumbling out of my mouth.

"You're crazy if you think any of this will have a happy ending."

"Back off! I know what I'm doing."

"There's a fucking drug lab downstairs!" I scream. "The people who're stealing our garbage aren't looking for our autographs. They're either going to kill us or slap us in prison. This has to stop!"

It's the conversation I've been afraid of having, and I've taken off the brakes, but it hasn't had any effect on him because I'm the only logical person in the room. Right now, the only thing I'm certain of is if Philip hadn't forgotten to refill his Valium prescription, our lives would be very different. He'd be the Philip I've always known. There wouldn't be a drug lab in the dungeon, and we wouldn't be on the radar of the burly guy and Guido and Little Louie.

The ten o'clock evening news is on television, and Philip has come up from downstairs and is standing in the middle of our bedroom. He hasn't said a word, but I can tell something's wrong.

"I'm dizzy, and my heart is pounding crazy fast."

He unbuttons his shirt so I can see his chest. His heart is vacillating back and forth like a can of Dove Gray paint in the mixing machine at Sherwin-Williams. *Tinkering, my ass!* I have no way of knowing how much coke he's snorted, but for Mr. "I've got it under control" to be standing here, it must be a lot.

He sits down on the sofa in front of the bedroom window, and just as quickly pops back up. I know he remembers what happened to our Hollywood friend, or he wouldn't be telling me this.

"I'm calling the EMS."

"No! Just sit with me." He points to the place next to him on the sofa.

"When's the last time you ate something?"

He shakes his head and shrugs his shoulders.

"Stay there. I'll be back in thirty seconds."

Like Philip, my heart is beating crazy fast but it's not from cocaine. I run to the kitchen and pour a big glass of milk and put a loaf of bread, the roast I fixed yesterday, a knife, and some mayonnaise on a tray, and take it back to the bedroom. I sit next to him on the sofa with the tray in my lap and hand him the milk.

"Drink it." I proceed to make him a roast beef sandwich.

"I'm not hungry."

"I don't care." My voice is calm but firm. He knows I'm not fooling around. "I'm hoping the food will absorb some of the coke in your system." I don't know if what I said is true, but unless he starts showing signs the food is helping, I'm calling the EMS.

I'll call for help, and he knows it. We've been here before. Like when he had a seizure after a week without his prescribed sleep medication. That time I'd called for help, and he wound up in the psych ward. And if I hadn't? In the *Physicians' Desk Reference*, the bible of prescription drugs and their side effects, death is listed as the last stage after seizures from abrupt Valium withdrawal.

He takes a bite of the sandwich and swallows some of the milk. "Just sit here with me. It won't happen again."

What a flipping fool I've been! If he dies, this will be my fault. I'll never be able to come to terms with my part in this. Every day I feel him slipping away, falling further down the rabbit hole with Alice and her friends to a place with a sign that says, "SNORT ME."

Sometimes Philip quotes Newton's third law of motion: "For every action, there is an equal and opposite reaction," and I know this to be true because nothing I've said has gotten through to him. It's just made me the enemy. Once again, I've role-reversed with someone important in my life, but the stakes are higher because it's no longer about the two of us. There are investors now and a company.

Philip's eating the sandwich and appears to be leveling out, and I take the opportunity to slip away and make a sweep of downstairs. In front of the door to the garage, there are the contents of six large boxes of nails, some of our racing trophies, a pile of gardening tools, and the box of BBs I scattered, and they're all just as I left them. I planted them in the hope our unwanted visitors would trip over them and alert me to their presence. On occasion, I've even nailed the doors shut that lead from the dungeon to the second floor to make it more difficult for them to get to us. How crazy does that make me? But I'm not crazy! I'm desperate! Desperate to trap Guido and Little Louie and the rest of the things down here that make the hair on my arms stand at attention.

CHAPTER FOURTEEN

I'VE BEEN WONDERING IF OUR UNWANTED VISITORS realize the vape's law firm has hired us a bodyguard—the sniper on the San Antonio SWAT squad—and if so, do they know he's not here all the time? Do they know I'm here much of the time alone? And if so, do they realize they're vulnerable as well? I know how to use a gun, and if it comes down to them or me, it's not going to be me. I've been pushed over an edge I didn't know existed, and I'm past hurt—I'm angry. The last thing I need is another push.

Philip and I walk the interior of the house with the bodyguard, and when we get downstairs, Philip explains the lab is related to the smokeless cigarette. I nod and smile as though everyone has a chemistry lab in their dungeon, except now I'm doing more than pretending. I'm lying to the police. Lying by omission, in hopes the rest of the SWAT squad doesn't descend on us in full force.

The bodyguard has checked the locks on the windows and doors on all three floors, and he's gone over our alarm system. "The guys who break into your house know what they're doing," he tells us.

Sometimes the bodyguard sits in his personal car in the Sam's Club parking lot across the street. From there he has a good view of the house, "the cherry on the sundae" as a friend

calls it because of the way it sits on top of twenty-two acres, isolated and away from the world around it. The bodyguard can
also see the entrance to our driveway at the foot of the hill. Other
times he leaves his car at Sam's Club and walks up the hill, or he
parks in our driveway and spends the night sitting in the shadows
on the veranda, watching and waiting and listening.

The first day he was here he told me, "Go about your life as
though I'm not here. Just act normal."

Normal. *Ha!* I can't remember the last time my life felt
normal. Even when I was a preteen, and then a teenager, none
of the other kids I knew took care of their mothers. Some
friends of ours have two kids, a Suburban, and the husband's
not making cocaine in the dungeon. That's normal.

It's challenging for me to act as though it's just another day
when I know there's a bodyguard outside waiting. It's the waiting
part that's unsettling, and it makes me feel anything but safe and
protected. More like one of those moving duck targets at the
county fair. Three shots for a dollar.

Tonight Philip, and the bodyguard, and I are taking a trial
run to a restaurant.

"I don't believe they'll try anything in public," he tells us,
"but you never know. Besides, if they want to harm you, they
couldn't ask for a more perfect place to make their move than
here at the house. It's remote, and there are so many covert ways
to get inside."

So far, I don't find him very reassuring.

Before we leave the house, the bodyguard opens his sports
jacket and shows us the side holster and the gun inside his coat.
Then he raises his slacks so we can see another gun strapped to
his leg.

"Nobody will know I'm carrying. I'll just be another guy
eating Chinese food."

Philip and I make small talk over kung pao chicken and Mongolian beef while the bodyguard sits at a table on the other side of the room and has egg rolls. He watches as the other customers come and go, and as the waitstaff delivers fried rice and moo shu pork, then clears the dishes and disappears through the swinging kitchen doors.

In case Guido and Little Louie saw us leave, we decide to go to the movies to give them plenty of time to break in. Philip and I sit in the middle of the theater while the bodyguard sits behind us in the last row. I don't need to look at him to know his eyes are trained on everything but the movie. That makes at least two of us.

This can't be our lives from here on out. Perhaps I can think of it as a passing phase like bell bottoms and double-breasted suits with shoulder pads. Next year everyone will be wearing a different fashion trend, and hopefully Philip and I will have our act together.

When we get back to the house, the bodyguard makes us wait on the veranda while he checks the perimeter and the inside. Then he escorts us indoors and accompanies us while we make sure nothing was disturbed while we were gone. Everything appears to be in order, but we're not any closer to knowing who's been overriding our alarm system and gaining entrance to our home, although there are only three candidates on my list: the DEA, the ATF, and the Big Six tobacco companies. And even though my husband's still making cocaine, I'm betting it's the tobacco companies. It's more in line with what I've learned about their style. They have a reputation for not playing nice, and they don't need a warrant.

I know this because from time to time, the former president of one of the world's largest tobacco companies calls me with tidbits for my vape diary. He's now FAVOR's vice president of marketing. This week he called with comments about the insidious relationship between the Feds and the executives who drive tobacco-colored Rolls-Royces. Powerful people who would like nothing more than for us to disappear from the face of the earth, but how far they're willing to go to stop us has yet to be determined.

Having a bodyguard and knowing there are forces with unlimited money and power who want to see us vanish without a trace is a scary way to live. Every day I'm forced to compartmentalize the dangerous things and put them on hold while the rest of me tries to believe Philip's the same man I fell in love with when inside, I know he's not. We're teetering on the edge of certain disaster, and somewhere in the back of my mind, I continue to hear the steady sound of a ticking clock.

Philip has raised a private placement of investor money, and he's brought on key employees. Together they've designed and purchased machines to manufacture the vapes. In addition, he's leased a large industrial space for the factory. How he's accomplished this while doing God knows how much cocaine and alcohol to bring him down, I'll never know.

In a few weeks the company's going public on the New York Stock Exchange, and one word from me—to anyone—would put everything in jeopardy. Daily I have conversations with myself: Do I continue to try and save my husband, or do what I can to ensure the company stays on track, because without FAVOR, where would he be? I think of it as his salvation and our way out, but it's almost like the chicken and the egg. Which came first?

I never think in terms of saving myself. It's always about him, and I vacillate from having hard conversations with him to pulling back and looking for other solutions. My voice comes and goes, but I've stopped judging myself. What I do isn't right or wrong. Normal or abnormal. It's just the way things are right now.

The other day, when we were in a meeting, FAVOR's Securities and Exchange Commission attorney said, "This would be fun if we knew how it turned out." It was an attempt to bring some levity to our needing a bodyguard and whether *they* will let us get away with bringing the smokeless cigarette to the marketplace. But he doesn't know about Philip's hobby in the dungeon and the slippery slope that continues to catapult us further down the rabbit hole.

The attorney's remark had tapped into the relentless checklist of dangerous scenarios that scroll through my mind on autopilot. I'd turned and looked him in the eye, and in all seriousness said, "What if we trade places? Let's give it a week. Then you can tell me which parts you think will be the fun ones."

CHAPTER FIFTEEN

FOR WEEKS, PHILIP HAS PICKED A FIGHT EVERY NIGHT after he gets home. Except for disputes about his drinking and using cocaine, in all the years we've been together, arguing's never been our style. Our disagreements always take me by surprise because they seem to erupt without warning. Regardless of what I say, he finds a way to twist my words in another direction, and the situation ratchets out of control before I can figure out how it began. Sometimes I wind up thinking I must be crazy! Maybe Mother and Philip and I will *all* wind up in the looney bin together.

Some nights a blowup starts—and I have no idea what triggered it—with something like, "You know exactly what I mean. It's like when you overcook the steak. How difficult is it to check it with a meat thermometer? Do you need me to show you, again?"

"But I thought we were talking about how the dry cleaner does the collars on your shirts, not how your steak is cooked."

Each argument scares me more than the one the night before because we're plunging further down a path that's nonnegotiable. To a place I don't recognize. Like a Stepford wife in careful subservience to her husband, I spend each day making sure every little thing is how he likes it. Then I wait in anticipation until he comes through the door.

When our exchanges are over, I've tried writing down our conversation so I could understand what happened, but the next day my words read like gibberish. It's like I'm living a page out of Abbott and Costello's "Who's on First?" except I can't grasp the conversation, much less find first base. I spend the rest of the day confused, wondering if the previous night was my fault. Some days I talk myself into believing I'm not sympathetic enough to the pressures he's under, the difficulties of navigating the legal landmines, and the challenges of getting the vape on the market. No one's done anything like this before. The possible pitfalls are colossal, and I know them all by heart, but I'm not the one on the front lines.

Other days, a part of me wants to say the man in my house is an impostor. He just *looks* like my husband. *This* man is touchy. About everything. He's not the Philip I know and love. That Philip's been gone for a while now.

Thinking about my role in this insanity and what I should do about it has taken over my waking hours. *Work harder today*, I tell myself. *Don't put pressure, of any kind, on him, and don't bring up his alcohol and cocaine usage.* But nothing helps. I'm clueless about what to do.

Except for our first ten years together, neither one of us has seen a happy marriage, but from the beginning I vowed to make this a good union. Over the years Philip's interests have become my interests, and I've subjugated my needs to be the woman he wants. I wanted to be the one woman he couldn't live without, but now I'm wondering if he's becoming the man I *can* live without. This isn't the first time I've come to this conclusion, and yet each time, it scares me to think it through. It fractures my heart and strips away everything I've loved about us.

I've always been more mature than my years. Sometimes I think I was born an adult. This would account for why Philip and I've never felt an age gap. We've been together since I was twenty-one, and now I wonder who I would be without him. I've asked myself this countless times, but I'm frozen in our toxic relationship, unable to think my way through it. Are there other women out there who are paralyzed by a similar poisonous relationship, and if so, how are they dealing with it?

Some nights Philip will come through the front door with a beaming smile, and I get my hopes up. He's animated and jovial, almost too jovial, and he says something like, "I've got a great story to tell you, but first I'm going to run downstairs and check on something I started in the lab this morning. I'll be back in a few minutes for dinner." But that never happens.

Dinner turns out to be a meal I eat by myself, and when he returns, I can tell he's had too much to drink and more than likely a lot of cocaine. His initial good mood, the one that suckered me in and made me hope *this* evening would be different, has changed into something and someone I don't recognize. He's no longer the happy, friendly guy who walked through the door. He's belligerent, eager to make me believe *I* am the one with the problem. This Philip scares me, but since he's never done anything to make me think I should be afraid of him, I tell myself I'm reading it all wrong.

This afternoon I've been trying to distract myself by doing the laundry. The washer and dryer are in a room downstairs behind the garage. I put the wet clothes in the dryer, but nothing happens when I press the power button. I check behind the dryer. The cord is plugged into the wall. Perhaps a fuse is blown.

The fuse box is hidden behind a trapdoor in the bathroom ceiling of the lab. When I lift away the small square door and turn on my flashlight, there, glittering in the beam of light are dozens of flask-sized empty bottles of vodka and at least ten big empty jugs of cheap red wine. My mouth drops open and I'm frozen in place, stunned by the sheer number of empty bottles wedged into this tiny space. The sight of them feels like I've been pushed off a cliff without a parachute, and my heart has landed in the pit of my stomach.

I've discovered the cause of his cheerful disposition when he comes home. He's riding the happy, talkative crest of a vodka wave: the half-pint of vodka I suspect he drinks each night on his way home from work, followed by at least another half-pint after he goes downstairs. I feel like I'm going to throw up when the definition of *crazy* hits me. It's a phrase I've heard all my life but until this moment, the meaning never applied to me.

Crazy is doing the same thing again and again and expecting different results. That's me! I've lost track of how many times I've asked Philip to stop drinking and using cocaine and yet, like a crazy person, I've continued to believe he would stop. Like last year when I talked him into seeking help. He stopped using cocaine and alcohol for more than a month, and then one morning, he told me he was done.

"I've tried it your way," he said. "The doctor I've been seeing is a quack! Yesterday, he pulled a bottle from a twisted brown paper sack in the bottom of his desk drawer. Then he held it up and said, 'Hell, we all need a crutch from time to time. Wanna join me in a drink?' And I'm taking advice from *this* guy?"

Philip and I had been standing in his dressing room as he got dressed to pitch a group of venture capitalists about investing in FAVOR.

"And the lithium, Mellaril, and chloral hydrate cocktail he put me on? I discovered he should've been monitoring me with multiple blood tests each week, but he just sent me on my way with something like, 'Keep me posted.'"

Philip had been adjusting his tie, but standing next to him, I could see he was angry.

"I've been on this stuff for a month. My tongue is thick, and I'm slurring my words. I can't raise money when I'm taking this stuff! Everyone will think I'm drunk, and I haven't had a drop! And no cocaine!"

I knew nothing about the diagnosis that came with the drug cocktail. I just knew my heart broke for him because he'd tried to stop. He'd done what I asked, and he'd tried. Really tried. Like his accidental withdrawal from Valium, once again, he'd been a victim of legal drugs and doctors who didn't explain the cautions that came with them.

"What if we find another doctor?" I'd asked.

"No! I'm done! I've tried it your way. Now I'm doing it my way."

As I stare at the empty bottles stashed in the small space around the fuse box, I realize what I'd already known but didn't want to admit. Philip's way had been to resume the vodka and cocaine.

He's too smart not to know the alcohol and cocaine are destroying him, and they're ruining our lives. He's no longer the handsome man I met with chiseled features and enough charisma and quiet confidence to wrap around the sun and jettison to the nearest star and back before anyone realized they were in the presence of a solar event. That man was nothing short of magical. This one looks bloated and grizzled. The results of a man at war with himself.

Sometimes I think the arguments are just an excuse for him to get mad and leave the house and go someplace where he can drink without feeling judged.

But every night I greet him at the door with a kiss and a hug as though the previous night never happened. I keep hoping for the best in light of everything I know to the contrary. Yes. I must be crazy, or at the very least, I'm doing something seriously wrong.

CHAPTER SIXTEEN

TONIGHT'S BLOWUP HAS ESCALATED OUT OF THIN AIR. Philip's shouting at me, but he's not making any sense, and his words aren't forming complete sentences. I'm not sure he's even speaking English.

Out of nowhere he throws me on the floor of his dressing room, and he drops down on top of me. His hands are around my throat, and he's choking me. He's lost in another world. I don't think he knows it's me!

I try and pry his hands away from my neck, but he's too strong. "Stop it!" I manage to spit out. "Stop!"

His hands have tightened around my neck, and we're staring at one another face-to-face. His eyes have gone black, and they have the blank vacant gaze of a shark. I'm terrified he's going to kill me. His face is distorted and surreal, like one of those Salvador Dalí paintings where the clocks are all bent and warped. I slap and claw at him, twisting back and forth, trying to wrestle myself out from under him.

I'm not sure how, but I'm on my feet, running the few steps to the bathroom. I close the door and reach to press the lock when I remember the new doorknob I installed doesn't have a lock. The doorknob with a lock was months on backorder, so I bought the one without.

On the other side of the door, I can hear Philip rustling through the drawers in his dressing room, and then outside the bathroom door, he fires a bullet.

Oh, God! Did he shoot himself?

He starts kicking the door with his foot and bellowing, "Open the door!" He, too, has forgotten the new doorknob doesn't have a lock, but for how long?

Other than standing here and waiting for him to get in, I have only one option. I shove open the second-story bathroom window and without hesitating, I leap into the night, hoping the tree outside will break my fall. I tumble down through a series of big branches and tree limbs. Sharp sticks and bark scrape and gouge at my flesh. I land, hard, at the base of the tree, then take off running down the backside of the property toward the wooded area behind the house.

My right ankle is in pain. I think I twisted it when I landed. The temperature is near freezing, and I'm wearing ballet slippers and a black lace bodysuit, but none of that matters. I run across the top of the hill, past the old red barn where sometimes I do photoshoots and portraits of friends. I stop just shy of the sharp drop-off on the backside of the hill. Unless I go back the way I came, there's no other place for me to go. I dive under a thorny pyracantha bush and make myself into a ball as small as possible.

Somewhere on the hill above me, I can hear Philip hollering, "I know you're out there!"

I can't tell if his voice is coming from the open second-story bathroom window or if he's outside and has followed my path down the hill toward the barn. He must know the barn would be one of the places I might go. I'm terrified of what he'll do if he finds me. *Please, don't let him find me.*

Twenty feet away, there's a bright overhead light that's hanging from the top of a tall cedar post. It's illuminating the ground around me, but it's too late for me to move. If he followed me, he might hear me or see me hiding under the bushes.

The thorns of the pyracantha feel like barbed wire, and they're gouging my arms, my back, and my scalp. I'm gasping for air, and with each heaving breath, the thorns plunge deeper into my flesh. I try and focus on my breathing. *In . . . out . . . slow . . . slow.* If I don't get my breathing under control, he'll hear me.

Above me, on top of the hill, I hear a tree limb break, and I will myself to be still. I've survived a lot of life-threatening things, and I've made it through to the other side of all of them. Starting when I was an Rh-negative baby, six weeks premature, and needed a complete blood transfusion the day I was born. Then there was the first time I had sex. I got pregnant. People say you always remember your first time, but all I remember is the illegal abortion.

It happened in one of those motels that scream low-rent and illegal. Matchbox bungalows separated by carports, window air conditioners, and patches of unpulled weeds. A clandestine structure, lurking in the afternoon shadows of an old Spanish mission. A Mexican woman who didn't speak English, who was part midwife and practiced witchcraft had prodded my vagina with a wire. For the next two days, I hemorrhaged in my childhood bedroom and hid the blood-soaked sanitary pads in a sack under my bed. If I could make it through that, I can make it through anything.

I've spent a lifetime pretending to be afraid of nothing and no one, but I never could have imagined I'd be terrified of the one person I've idolized and adored my entire adult life. There have been other nights when the cocaine and alcohol made him crazy, but tonight, he might as well have gone ahead and killed me because emotionally, I feel wounded beyond repair.

I haven't moved a muscle since I dove headfirst into the

brush, and I don't know how long I've been in this position. An hour, maybe two. Long enough for the deer to walk past me like I'm part of the landscape. It's started to rain, but the deer next to me don't seem to notice. I'm terrified to get up and walk back to the house. Afraid of what I might find. *What if he trashed the house or hurt himself?* This time I won't blame myself. I didn't make him do this terrible thing.

Things go south almost every night, but not like this. I've never seen him this blitzed. I think he could have killed me and not remembered it in the morning. I'm shaking from fear and the freezing cold, but the realization the man I fell in love with—the one I respected and revered—tried to kill me, jolts me with an even bigger chill.

I'm cold and wet, and my arms and legs are cramped, but I disentangle myself from the pyracantha and crawl out from under the brush. My bodysuit is torn, my skin is bloodied, and there are sticks in my hair. Things like this aren't supposed to happen to women like me. I'm educated, a woman of means, married to a brilliant and prominent man, but I get it now.

Addiction is education- and income-agnostic. All this time, I thought I was shielding him from the public consequences of accidentally running out of Valium—just until he pulled himself together—and now his drinking and using cocaine. But in shielding him from any accountability, I've made matters worse.

I retrace my steps up the hill and pause to peer around the corner of the garage. His car is gone. The winding front steps, the ones the big burly weightlifter took two at a time, are slick and wet from the rain, and the front door is wide open, waiting for everything to start all over again tomorrow.

CHAPTER SEVENTEEN

PHILIP'S BEEN GONE ALL NIGHT. HE HASN'T CALLED. I haven't heard from the police, and I'm angry and relieved at the same time. Part of me wants to interpret this as a good sign, but there's nothing good about any of this. We can never reset to zero, and I don't know where we go from here.

Today all I've done is sit on the sofa in front of the bedroom window. It's a grey day outside, cold and rainy. I've wrapped myself in a blanket, but inside I'm cloaked in this sick feeling of dread. I can't stop imagining something terrible has happened to him or been caused by him. If he could savagely attack me, then maybe he could do the same thing to someone else. I will never forget the feel of his hands around my throat. How his rage and the drugs changed him not just on the inside but his outward appearance as well.

All this time, I thought he would find his way out of the maze of addiction and return to being the brilliant entrepreneur with his finger on the pulse of the times: the personal computer, the microprocessor, the smokeless cigarette. Maybe if I'd understood how powerless I'd been to get him to stop, I could have taken a different tactic, but I don't know what it would have been.

I've watched every car get off the freeway, hoping, and fear-ing, his car will be one of them. I'm unable to think about or do anything else, because if I leave my seat in front of the window, there's a chance I won't see him come up the driveway, and I need to be ready in case I have to run. But then, where would I go? I have no cash and no credit cards, and I can't go to a friend's house. Most of them are involved with the company in some way, and I can't tell any of them about last night.

Then again, maybe I should be the one to leave and let him come home to an empty house and wonder what happened to me. If I'm all right. If something terrible happened to me. I could get in my car and watch our driveway from the Sam's Club's parking lot across the street like the bodyguard does. My silver Porsche with the flared fenders is hardly low-profile, but then neither is my house nor the man I married. Yes. We would make for splashy stories at six and ten on the evening news.

Somehow I managed to fall asleep, and when I wake it's dark outside. I hear voices in the living room. Philip is sitting in his corner of the sofa with some sleazeball at the other end, talking like they're old friends. I'm guessing it's someone he met at a scuzzy neighborhood bar. Someone who won't judge him. Someone who will be impressed that his fellow addict lives in one of the most famous houses in Texas and has two Porsches and a Mercedes with heated seats and a sunroof.

I'm angry! Oh, let me count the ways I'm angry! He could have killed me, and he's been gone for twenty-four hours, leaving me to wonder and worry about him. But more than that, he's endangered me for longer than I want to admit, and now he's brought a seedy stranger into my home.

I bite my tongue and walk past them like they aren't there. I want Philip to know I've seen his two-bit panhandler friend. I wonder if he's given him a tour of the lab downstairs or shown him the secret wall safes and the hidden room upstairs?

What does he think will happen if this guy tells one of his degenerate buddies about his new friend who lives in the infamous Spy House on the Hill? What if they come back with guns to rob us or to blackmail him? Then we'll have a whole new cast of characters to add to our existing nightmare. More guys for me to fear other than Guido and Little Louie and now the man I married.

We haven't had any more arguments, and neither one of us has said a word about the other night. I'm terrified to bring it up because I don't know what might trigger him and result in another confrontation. Now I'm the one who's become the mannequin in the darkened room.

With every thought and emotion and with each word that comes out of my mouth, I'm treading water, trying to fly under the radar so there's nothing he can latch onto and use to start a fight. But soon I'm going to need to feel solid ground beneath my feet. The security that comes with knowing he won't leave and stay away all night, or that I won't have to flee down the hill and hide behind the dumpster at the convenience store half a mile away. Yes. I've done that too, but I won't admit it to anyone.

Except for going to the office, Philip hasn't left the house. Some days he appears to be okay, but most of the time I can tell he's depressed. Alcohol, and lots of it, has become his sleep elixir, but I don't think he's using cocaine because the craziness isn't there. I want to interpret this as a good sign, but he's far from all right and neither am I. I'd like to let my guard down and fall asleep, confident the house won't blow up, but I'm afraid to go to sleep before he does. Sometimes I fake sleep, hoping he'll finally have enough to drink and pass out.

Most days, like today, I sit here on the sofa, staring out of the bedroom window, wondering if the events of the other night will start all over again. I've replayed every detail in my mind. I think about leaving him, but without me here as his "watcher," what if he slips over the edge and destroys himself? I don't want that for him or me, and if I leave, where would I go? What would I do?

It's taken all my courage and determination to stay in this marriage. Sometimes I wonder why I'm still here, but my answer is always the same: I stay because I've loved him since the moment I realized he was special. I stay because he needs me. I stay because without me, I fear the house could explode and rain down chunks of his legacy and reputation like pieces of an angry, white-hot volcano. But the one thing I keep coming back to is, I don't have any money.

The Porsche I drive is not in my name, and any chance of having a career has been sidetracked by his out-of-control train. But I've let it happen. What I don't know is whether Philip would give me any money until I find a job, or if he would talk about a separation, and how that conversation would go. I do know I don't want to talk to him about it alone, and at the same time, I want to believe he's going to pull himself out of the abyss. That life will go back to the way it was before the project in the dungeon, but I can't let myself buy into such shaky rationale because I've come to understand addiction.

Addiction grabs you by the jugular vein and won't let go. It erases all memories of love and shame and a normal life. The only thing an addict cares about is getting more of what's taking them down. Their drug becomes their new family, their best friend, and their lover, and the need for more is hardwired into their brain. Welded into their heart and soul is a protective cage that keeps their addiction in and everyone else out. I've decided it would be easier to stitch sequins around the moon than to get an addict to stop using their drug of choice.

I pick up the framed photograph on the table next to me. It's one of my favorites, the two of us a few months after we moved in together. It's easy to see we were in love, but now all I see is a twenty-one-year-old woman who was ripe for the picking by an older man. A glamorous James Bond type with Top Secret clearance. A man who built hush-hush black boxes for the government, the telemetry systems for the Titan and Atlas rockets, and had a torrid love affair in Paris with a beautiful Russian spy.

Did he choose me because he thought he could mold me into the woman he wanted? I thought I'd made myself into that woman, the one he couldn't walk away from, but in the end, what does it matter? Whether he molded me, I molded myself, or I gave up my free will and allowed him to do it? All I wanted was to be loved, but the result is still the same: I've abandoned myself to be loved by a man I no longer recognize.

Idolatry's a lot like sterling silver. Over time both of them tarnish, except silver can be polished until the dark and grimy bits are gone, but people are different. Once they've lost their luster you can buff them up again, but deep down you know it's like dressing paper dolls. Even if you fold all the tabs flat against the back of the doll, it's only a matter of time before you realize you've dressed a pig in a ballgown.

CHAPTER EIGHTEEN

AFTER MY FIRST HIGH SCHOOL REUNION, A GIRLFRIEND later told me that when I'd walked in with Philip Ray, everyone had stopped and paused to stare at us.

"You were there with a man," she said. "But we were there with boys."

I suspect it was more than the fabulous-looking man on my arm that surprised them. I looked nothing like the girl they'd known in high school. Gone were the thick glasses—in favor of contact lenses—as well as the fifteen pounds I gained the summer between my junior and senior years. Mother and I had clashed over everything that summer, and I'd sought refuge in the dough balls I made and ate like jellybeans. Slices of white bread, minus the crust, I rolled in my hands until they had the consistency of glutinous bread dough.

The night of the reunion I wore a slim, white silk shirtdress that buttoned down the front and came to just above my knees and a pair of pale peach snakeskin heels with a tiny strap that buckled around my ankles. The label on the outside of the shoe-box read, "Tuscan Mousse." Funny, the things I remember. Philip wore a dark grey tailored suit, a dress shirt and tie, and a pair of thin-soled black Bally slip-ons. If my classmates had looked closer, they would have noticed our matching black Movado watches we'd exchanged instead of traditional wedding rings. The large museum piece for him and the smaller one for me.

While my outward appearance had changed, inside I'd become a different person as well. I was confident and fearless, used to risking everything for the momentary thrill of a new adventure which then seamlessly became a part of me. Whether we were racing cars, scuba diving, exploring jungles and unpaved backroads in Third World countries, or our room for the night was a hammock with a skinned squirrel that dripped blood on our foreheads, it wasn't long before I felt like a Bond girl, dressed in a white bikini with a dive knife strapped to my leg.

Since the first day we started seeing one another, I've done almost everything Philip wanted without allowing myself to think much beyond the face value of his request. I never wanted to disappoint him, and if anything raised a red flag, I turned my back on it and told myself I was brave and adventurous. A risk-taker. A reflection of him. A sophisticated mate for a worldly man. I was more than arm candy.

But of all the daredevil things I've done, hanging onto Philip's out-of-control train may be the most difficult one of all. I'm still the woman who craves adventure, but instead of being an active participant in my life, all I do is wait for the next crisis. This morning I decided to change all of that.

"I want to work for the company." I say it before I had a chance to think about it. Next month, he's taking FAVOR public on the New York Stock Exchange, and there are plenty of positions to fill and things to be done.

He knows I'm more than qualified, but he looked me in the eye and said, "It wouldn't look right for my wife to work for the company." It was the end of the conversation.

When I think about it, I know he's right, but it does little to mitigate my disappointment. I know more about nicotine, the

Big Six, the ATF, and the legal conundrum the smokeless cigarette faces than almost anyone except Philip and the attorneys.
My research has laid the groundwork for numerous teams of
lawyers, and I've cowritten the business plan. No one knows the
extent of my behind-the-scenes involvement but the two of us.
I'm a researcher, business partner, and devil's advocate, not to
mention I've worked for three of his other companies.

In the early years at Datapoint, I was the entire accounts
payable department, plus I handled the accounts of companies
that leased Datapoint's computer terminals like Texas Instru-
ments, IBM, Honeywell, Pillsbury, and TRW. Mr. Ray and I
seldom crossed paths, and I'd worked there a year and a half
before we had a real conversation. A chance encounter at the
company's after-work watering hole had been the beginning of
our relationship.

We clicked, and we knew it. He was newly divorced and
when he walked me to my car, he held the door open and said, "I
won't date employees." The next day I handed in my resignation,
and two weeks later, we were living together.

It wasn't long before Philip made me the chief operating
officer of a company in which he was an investor. It was just me
and the guys in manufacturing. I handled the front office, did
the accounting, made cold calls to Gibson's, JCPenney, and
Sears, and sold thousands of greenhouses their customers could
put together by themselves. Easy as one, two, three. Then there
was the Valium incident when I made myself the de facto president of his second high-tech startup. While he recovered, I
soothed anxious investors, made fiscal decisions, and learned
more about advanced computer memory than I dreamed of
knowing.

In all our years together, I've set any semblance of a career
aside to be the woman Philip needed. Just once I'd like a *Thank*

you, or a *What would I do without you?* But right now, I'll let it go. For him.

The book on my dressing table is the latest in a long line of books I've read about addiction. I could have written the chapter called Spouses: *It's not uncommon for sober spouses to stay in an unhealthy marriage. They often need as much help as the addict.* I think it means I'm on the same shaky tightrope because I see myself on every page. I've covered for him and pleaded with him to stop using, but I haven't set healthy boundaries or let him suffer the consequences of his drug use. Maybe he's afraid I would do that if I worked for the company, or without meaning to, I would make our private problems public.

Once again I've put the needs of my husband over my own. Gloria Steinem and the other feminists of my generation would be disappointed to learn I've chosen a man with a drug problem over a career. I've abandoned myself and surrendered my power, and if I have any chance of surviving this nightmare, I need to find something that doesn't include Philip and cocaine or vapes and bodyguards.

Philip has to know I'm close to throwing in the towel because yesterday he threw me a bone.

"Why don't you contact the Air Force and tell them you'll give them some good publicity in return for a ride in one of their jets?"

At the time his suggestion felt like a consolation prize, but the more I've thought about it, I realize it's a great fit. I'm a good writer. I'm adventurous, and I like to watch the Air Force fighter jets do touch-and-go landings through the telescope in our living room. Okay, Philip. I'm done feeling trapped and out of options. I'll take your bone.

CHAPTER NINETEEN

I CAN HEAR THE VOICE IN THE CONTROL TOWER THROUGH the headphones inside my flight helmet. "Reno Three-Zero, you're cleared for takeoff." I'm strapped into the rear seat of a US Air Force T-38, a sleek two-seater version of the F-5A fighter jet, for an article I'm writing for *Southwest Airlines Magazine*. It's my first step toward reclaiming my power and my independence.

"Okay, Brenda. That's us. You ready?" Colonel Carter's in the front seat, a Vietnam veteran and the Air Force instructor pilot who's taking me up.

"I am! Let's do this!" It's time to see if I have the "right stuff." If the right stuff is swallowing my fears while living with a brilliant man who often borders on madness then, yes. I've had the right stuff for longer than I care to admit.

My helmet's connected to an oxygen mask. I'm wearing a khaki green Air Force flight suit with the squadron's patch on the sleeve, regulation boots, and a pair of fireproof gloves. There's a parachute buckled to the back of my suit, and I'm sitting on an ejection seat I hope I don't have to use.

"Here we go!" the Colonel declares. "I'll light the afterburners."

The jet gathers speed like it's been flung out of a giant slingshot, and we're zooming past massive airplane hangars so fast they look like they're the size of tiny matchboxes. The other jets on the runway are a blur, and somewhere back there with the ground crew, Philip and our friend, Rick, are watching.

"Gears up. Flaps up, and we're airborne!" the Colonel announces. "We're pulling up pretty good now. Can you feel it?"

I answer "Roger!" but what I really want to say is "Holy shit!" We're streaking through the south Texas sky as fast as lightning lights up the wild blue yonder. Overhead the cockpit's canopy is clear, and I can see in every direction for what appears to be hundreds of miles.

"There's San Antonio over there to the right, Brenda. You want a better look at the Tower of the Americas?" The Colonel executes a 90-degree snap roll to the right, and in a blink, the jet's wings are perpendicular to the Earth. "There it is."

The rapid change of position reminds me I'm not wearing a G-suit. They didn't have one small enough to fit me, which means it will be easier for me to get airsick and blackout—an indignity I'm determined to avoid. I'm reminded of the first time I went scuba diving. Every piece of my gear felt foreign and uncomfortable, and like my first time in the ocean, I've promised myself I won't complain. No matter what.

"We're going 300 knots, Brenda. Wanna go 400?"

The acceleration is exhilarating, faster than anything I've experienced racing cars, and the only sound I hear is the Colonel's breathing and mine through the headphones. In front of me, there's an array of red, black, and yellow knobs along with switches and gauges all screaming, "Do Not Touch on Penalty of Death."

"How about a couple of G-forces?"

"Let's do it!" I've already experienced G-forces in a clipped-wing Super Cub stunt plane, and I've ridden in the front seat of a sailplane—a plane with no engine that glides like a bird on the wind until it finds a safe place to land before the wind disappears.

"There's two Gs. Now four," the Colonel says. The jet continues to accelerate nose first, straight up, through endless white castles in the sky. "Did that black ya out?"

The G-forces have pushed my head into my lap; my eyelids are somewhere down around my knees, and I'm working hard to keep from passing out.

I'm still recovering from staring at my inseams when the Colonel offers a hearty, "Wanna go straight down? That's straight down, Brenda! Look at the ground."

Everything's happening so fast, and other than being worried about passing out, I don't have time to be scared. I raise my head in time to see us barreling, nose-first, toward postage stamp-sized farms and tiny teardrop lakes and rivers that meander through the countryside. Hondo, Texas, is rapidly becoming too up-close and personal.

"Wanna go fast, Brenda? Let's go fast. When the gauge gets to one, we'll be supersonic!" The Colonel is having a blast, showing me what his baby can do. "That's almost six Gs, Brenda! What do you think?"

"Heavy," I manage to say. "Yeah, let me . . ." My voice trails off. "Just for a little while."

"Turn up the oxygen. It'll make ya feel better."

My article and several full-page photographs of me in a flight suit sitting in an Air Force fighter jet appeared in this month's *Southwest Airlines Magazine*. I'm amazed how many people we know have called to say they read it. Such a kick! I've missed having a sense of accomplishment and independence.

Friends tell me Philip carries the magazine in his briefcase and shows it to everyone who enters his office. They say he's proud of me, but I would rather hear this from him. I'm reminded of my father who never praised me but expected me to excel at everything. How can men be so clueless? Or is it a power thing?

The Army, the Navy, and the Marines have all read the *Southwest* article and have called and asked if they have any toys I'd like to play with. Last week I became the first journalist to drive and fire the Army's M-1 Abrams tank. Next month I'm scheduled to do a cable-arrested landing and a catapult takeoff from an aircraft carrier and submerge in a nuclear submarine.

While I'm having a blast, it's occurred to me my adventures are reflections of the highwire acts at home—dangerous and full of adrenaline. A friend has started calling me Ramborella: part Rambo and part Barbarella, the beautiful, badass iconic sex goddess. At least it's an identity that's separate and apart from my husband.

The editor-in-chief of *Southwest Airlines Magazine* has asked me to meet him for lunch. "I have your check and a copy of the magazine with your latest article." He tells me he wants me to do more first-person adventure pieces. "You should see the letters to the editor I've gotten. Southwest Airlines passengers are eating this up."

After lunch, as we stand on the front steps of the restaurant, he takes me by the shoulders and bulldozes my mouth with his tongue.

"Our readers aren't the only ones who could eat you up."

I haven't done anything to make him believe I would welcome a move like this. I'm caught off-guard, and all I can think of to say is, "Shame on you." But I know it's shame on me for not telling him he's a jackass. My new career has blown up in my face.

I finally get what "pay to play" means, and inside, a part of me dies. Instead of finding another magazine to write for, I've taken myself out of the game. It's not just a career opportunity that's been squashed. I'm depressed and back to where I started. I have nothing of my own.

CHAPTER TWENTY

WE'VE MOVED THE BLACK L-SHAPED SOFA AGAINST the wall and Alan, Philip's boyhood friend, is unfolding a giant map of the Amazon River across our living room floor. Alan is obsessed with looking for a legendary emerald mine that allegedly borders the 10,000-acre cattle ranch he once owned in Colombia.

"I want you to come with me," he tells us. "You're the only people I know who've slogged your way through the jungle."

This isn't the first time Alan has asked us to come with him. Over the years he's told us stories about the elusive emerald mine, what it was like to live in Columbia, and the hazards of bringing his cattle to market.

Alan points to a spot on the map. "Not long ago, Texaco built a road, right through here." He pauses to look first at me and then Philip. "And if I'm right, we won't have to trudge through this part of the jungle, because we'll be able to see the mountain range in question from the road. That's great news!"

Alan's only talking about a scouting trip to see how far the road goes and to get a feel for what it would take to mount a full-blown expedition, but I know Philip isn't physically up to the trek. Out of the corner of my eye I glance at him, trying to get a read on what he's thinking. He's got to know he's not up for a trip like this, but neither one of us say a word about it. Instead, we tell Alan we'll go with him. I'm not sure why Philip agreed, but I agreed because my little voice tells me the man who binges on cocaine and vodka will never make it as far as South America.

I'm the first to get my shots—hepatitis A and B, typhoid, yellow fever, malaria, and tetanus—the vaccines we'll need before venturing into the tributaries of the Amazon. Once before, when the three of us talked about making this trip, I read up on the kind of things we'd encounter. The Amazon River and the surrounding jungle are teeming with insect, food, and waterborne diseases. And if those aren't crippling enough, the Amazon is full of scary creatures like tertiary yaws, microscopic survivors from the Cenozoic Era that bore into the soft tissue of human feet, often causing spontaneous amputation of the toes.

There aren't many people who would agree, even in principle, to go on such a trip, and I understand. I never expected to thrive on, and crave, living on the edge. It happened over time before I knew how much I liked it and wanted to do it again. Thrill-seeking is a tenuous thread that dangles from the polar opposite of normal, whatever normal is. I've never had a sense of what it's like to have children and attend family dinners and belong to the PTO. And while it's probably too late for me to become mainstream, my normal is gravitating toward those with common experiences like mine, and right now that's Alan.

When it's Philip's turn to get his shots, I ask Simon, our doctor, if he'll give him a physical as long as he's here. "Who knows when you'll get another chance."

An hour passes before Philip appears in the doorway of the waiting room. "Something showed up on my chest X-ray. Simon's sending me next door for a biopsy."

Something showed up on my chest X-ray. Philip might as well have dropped a bomb in the room because as sure as I'm sitting here, life as we know it has just exploded. It's what my little voice has been telling me for some time now: Philip's not in good health.

Next door to Simon's office is a hospital. The corridor outside the operating room is cold and dark, and it matches my mood. I'm anxious and scared of what the surgeon will discover. An hour goes by before Simon comes out and finds me.

"The biopsy results will be in later today, but during the procedure, his left lung collapsed. It's not uncommon in a lung biopsy. He's been admitted to the hospital, and they've taken him to a room on the fifth floor."

A few hours later, Simon and two doctors we've never seen are standing in Philip's hospital room. Their smiles are mirror images of ours, forced and awkward, and I know, before they say anything, the news isn't good.

"Your left lung and some of the lymph nodes in the medi-astinum, the area at the top of the chest and the base of your throat, have tested positive for cancer," one of them says. "You have stage IV adenocarcinoma of the lung."

They might as well be speaking Swahili. "What does stage IV mean?" I ask.

"Later this afternoon, an oncologist will stop by and talk to you about it." It's the only answer they will give me. Philip hasn't said a word.

Our world has been condensed onto a pathology slide, two inches long and three-quarters of an inch wide. Philip has lung cancer. I'm terrified and in shock, and Philip is mute. On my list of heinous things to worry about, lung cancer wasn't in any of the columns, and I feel guilty for toppling the first domino. For asking Simon to give him a physical.

While one of the doctors checks the small plastic tube they've inserted into Philip's chest to inflate his lung, I wrestle with the implications of his diagnosis. I vacillate between wondering if lung cancer is curable, and if not, how long does he have? As I struggle to keep my fears at bay, I'm hoping someone will come in and tell us they read the wrong pathology report.

We're sorry. It was all an unfortunate mistake. And if it's a mistake, Philip will value it as an opportunity to fight his way through the slipstream of addiction and start over again.

The oncologist looks young enough that Philip could be his first patient. He has that fresh-out-of-med-school look with his Hippocratic Oath saddled to a deer caught in the headlights. I hope he's up on state-of-the-art lung cancer treatment.

"There's a paper in this month's *Journal of Oncology* about your type and stage of cancer," he says. I've been told he knows Philip by reputation, and he treats him with a deference that signifies he's in the company of a brilliant mind. "I thought you might benefit from reading this. I'll stop by later and we can discuss it further."

As soon as he leaves, Philip opens the journal and begins reading. His expression is stone-faced, but in less than a minute, he closes the journal and sails it across the room like a frisbee. The pages land in my lap.

"Do what you think is best," he says.

I've read enough scientific papers to know the first paragraph is usually a summation of the rest of the article, but like Philip, it's difficult for me to read past the first sentence:

Regardless of the treatment protocol, the five-year survival rate for patients with stage IV adenocarcinoma of
the lung is less than ten percent.

If that isn't bad enough, it says the brain is one of the first
places lung cancer can metastasize. They've already told us the
lymph nodes in Philip's neck are overflowing with cancer cells,
and it's not a leap to imagine some of the deadly cells are already
there. *Cancer in his brilliant brain.*

The words in the oncology journal feel like another gut
punch, and I let the journal drop from my hands. *Terminal cancer . . .* It's all so final and surreal. I'm working hard to keep my
fears and emotions in check. I'm scared and out of my element,
but this isn't about me and my fears. It's about my husband.

I look across the room at Philip. His face is inscrutable,
absent of an expression of any kind. A myriad of questions are
racing through my mind. *Is he surprised by the diagnosis? Is he
afraid? And the vape . . . Did it contribute to his lung cancer, or is
it one piece of a puzzle that began when he started smoking at
fifteen? And what about the fumes in the lab and the chemical
spill on his leg?*

A nurse enters the room and begins taking his temperature
and blood pressure. He smiles at her as though everything is
right with the world. *Typical,* I think. He stopped sharing his
thoughts when the cocaine and the alcohol escalated, and now,
by how he's interacting with the nurse, I know he's walled himself and his diagnosis off from me and any questions I might
have.

I'm on my own and the oncology journal has robbed me of
any illusions I might have about a cure. I watch him smile at the
nurse, and a twinge of jealousy stabs at my heart. She's getting to
see the man I haven't seen in a long time. His cancer journey has

just begun, but I ache with grief, as though we've been on this road for as long as I can remember.

Tears collect along my lower eyelids, but they're not what he needs from me. If I'm going to help him get through this, I need to shut down my feelings and my fears like he has. I need to be the researcher I've always been and come back to him with some possible next steps.

My only experience with cancer was with my father. I was twelve, and no one told me what kind of cancer he had, but by the time he was diagnosed, it was too late to do anything. According to what I've read in the journal, it's too late for Philip as well.

The nurse has left the room, and Philip's polite smile has disappeared as quickly as if he'd turned off a light. He closes his eyes like he's going to sleep, and his solemn reclusive demeanor makes it clear he's not interested in having a conversation with me.

I replay his words in my mind. "Do what you think is best." They're hard to misinterpret.

As far back as when he was in high school, Philip was the person people looked to for answers, and I think about the comment a classmate wrote in his yearbook: *If the world is coming to an end, I'll beat a path to Philip Ray's door because he'll figure a way out of it.*

The man who would find a way out of most anything has withdrawn and given the job to me. Perhaps it's because taking charge is something I've done since childhood, but this day feels like it was inevitable.

CHAPTER TWENTY-ONE

I MAY HAVE TABLED MY EMOTIONS, BUT IT FEELS LIKE I'm sleepwalking my way through a bad dream. While Philip is sleeping off the anesthesia from his biopsy, I've taken the oncology journal and met our friend Stephen at the medical school library. If Philip won't have a conversation about his cancer with me, Stephen will, and like Philip, Stephen is brilliant.

We find a couple of empty chairs next to one of the library's computers, and I do a cursory search for "stage IV adenocarcinoma of the lung" and "treatment protocols."

Stephen and I flag any references that might contain useful information or something that will lead us to the top experts in lung cancer. We split the list and begin pulling journals and medical books from the library shelves, and when one of us finds a treatment or an interesting study, we share it with the other. Sometimes it leads us to other references, but each one turns out to be as depressing as the last, and the outcomes are all the same: The five-year survival rate for patients with stage IV adenocarcinoma of the lung is not good.

"There's no magic formula is there?" My tears have started, and it's the first time since Philip's diagnosis this morning I've allowed myself to give in to the reality of what he's facing. "He won't be here this time next year, will he?"

"We don't know that." Stephen's eyes have tears in them as well. He reaches for the paper where I've been writing down the names of leading cancer researchers and oncologists. Two are in Houston. "What if we pay these guys a visit? We have nothing to lose."

Several young med students walk past us. They're laughing and jovial, oblivious to our pain. I can't imagine ever being that happy or carefree again. Like rats snared in a trap, our future has snapped down on us without warning.

It's raining when Stephen and I leave the Houston airport and pull up in front of Dr. Polinski's building. The doctor's expecting us. He unlocks the front door, and we step inside and exchange introductions.

"What kind of cancer does your husband have?" he asks me.

"Stage IV adenocarcinoma of the lung. My friend and I read where you're doing some promising studies with lung cancer patients."

"They're more than promising, Mrs. Ray. My patients are being cured! Let's talk while I give you a tour. You're going to be very impressed."

Dr. Polinski's building is sleek and modern and smells like it's brand-new. As we walk, I notice the other half of the building is in total darkness. The weather forecasters have warned that Houston's in the path of a bad storm, and I think nothing of darkened building. Perhaps the lightning has tripped a circuit breaker.

"We've just received our new equipment," Dr. Polinsky says. He opens the door to one of the labs and turns on the lights. "See for yourselves. It's all very exciting!"

If I let myself, it would be easy to get caught up in the doctor's enthusiasm. At the very least, it might give me a much-needed shot of hope.

Inside the room is a glistening new laboratory outfitted with state-of-the-art vent hoods, a cryogenic freezer, and sparkling glass beakers. He closes the door and shows us another room further down the hall, and when he turns on the lights it looks exactly like the first lab, but there are no employees. No researchers. No patients. Not even a receptionist in the lobby. If I had to guess, I'd say we're the only people in the building.

"Your setup's very impressive," Stephen says. "But we want to know more about the work you're doing to see if you can help Mrs. Ray's husband."

"If Mrs. Ray writes me a check for $60,000, I will cure her husband of his cancer!"

Stephen and I have read dozens of medical studies, but nowhere did we see the words *cure* and *stage IV lung cancer* together. Dr. Polinski's statement is off-the-wall outrageous, and I reign in the urge to call him a scam artist.

Instead, I say, "May we see the data from your work?"

"Do you doubt me? Do you want me to cure your husband or not?"

Polinski is framed by the doorway of his new research lab. His head is tilted back, and he's staring down at me like I'm some kind of bug under a magnifying glass.

"Where are your lab technicians?" I ask. "It looks like your labs have never been used."

"Before I can continue, I need funding for my research."

Like everything else that's come out of his mouth, Polinski's statement is beyond offensive. I wanted hope, but he's selling me false hope. Part of me wants to slap the smug, self-important look off his face. Does he believe I would write him a check for that much money based on nothing but his claim he can cure my husband? Stephen and I can't get out of there fast enough.

Outside in the rental car, we sit in silence. The heavy rain is pelting the roof with short staccato bursts. They sound as angry as I feel.

"How many people do you suppose fall for that pitch?"

Stephen's as outraged as I am. "Enough to have built and outfitted a brand-new building. Desperate people do desperate things."

"Do you suppose he's even a doctor? Or a real researcher?" I sit and ponder the notion that in addition to being a conman, he may be a quack. "I'm reminded of an article I read about actor Steve McQueen. Like Philip, McQueen had stage IV lung cancer, and when his oncologists couldn't do anything for him, he checked himself into a spa for a series of unorthodox cancer treatments." With my fingers, I put air quotes around the word *spa*.

"The *spa* was in Juarez, Mexico, and it was run by an orthodontist. A dentist who corrects crooked teeth! The guy was a total charlatan. He didn't have a lab, not even an x-ray machine, but he took Steve McQueen's money."

My body's begun to shake, and it's from more than being cold and wet from the rain. My anger has spilled over, not just for Philip and me, but for Steve McQueen and all the other vulnerable cancer patients and their families who are desperate for a cure. I'm mad and heartbroken over every sad, and yet, hopeful day until those with advanced cancer take their last breath, and the ones left behind lose the people they love.

"Did he help him?"

"The quack at the spa? No, but every day he gave McQueen codeine, a sauna, a coffee enema, and an injection of apricot pits. No. . . Philip will not be anyone's *spa* patient!"

By the time we drive the short distance to MD Anderson

and park, I've calmed down. At least we know the cancer center and the oncologist we're meeting are world-renowned.

Just as Stephen and I expected, the oncologist tells us, "There's no cure for stage IV lung cancer, but there are new ways to see if the chemotherapy is working. They can help us tailor our treatment in hopes of buying more time. There's a promising study at the National Cancer Institute, outside of Washington, D.C. that delivers targeted therapy to the cancer cells but leaves the healthy cells alone. If you'd like, I can get your husband into their study."

Pending Philip's approval, and that of his oncologist in San Antonio, we agree on a game plan: MD Anderson will work with Philip's oncologist to develop and administer a treatment protocol, and a week after each chemotherapy, I will drive him the 200 miles to MD Anderson for tests to see how the chemo is working. I have no false hopes. I'm only buying time until a miracle occurs, or I get a glimpse of the man I fell in love with, and Philip remembers him, too.

On the flight back to San Antonio, I'm flooded with memories of the first time I saw him. The only words that came to mind that day were "gorgeous" and "magnetic." Until then, I thought men like him were only in the movies. He was tall and thin, a mixture of hip Clint Eastwood and a young Gary Cooper.

His hair was long and blond and flipped up on the edge of his collar. Neat and well-kept, in style with the times—the Seventies. Two Mickey Mouse ears were peeking out from under the French cuffs of his shirt. A dress shirt and a Mickey Mouse watch were an intriguing but unlikely pairing.

More than a year later, we ran into one another at the Turtle Creek Country Club after work, and he'd taken an empty seat on the barstool next to me. It was the first time we'd spoken since the office Christmas party six months before. His shirtsleeves were rolled midway to his elbows, and I'd held up my wine glass and nodded in the direction of his bare wrist. "Is Mickey Mouse underage?"

He'd laughed and asked, "You like Mickey Mouse?"

"Of course! He's an icon. Mickey Mouse and Marilyn Monroe. They're timeless."

Our conversation was fun and easy like we'd known one another forever, and we'd talked about everything from movies and hot air balloons to the design of the nautilus shell. Occasionally someone from the company stopped by to say hello to him, and most of them said the same thing: "I don't see you here very often."

Instead of responding with an answer about himself, he'd replied with something about them like, "Is that your Mustang I saw in the parking lot?"

I remember listening to the easy way he talked with people and the congenial but respectful way they responded. It was obvious he was held in high esteem, and he was nothing like my preconceived notion of the president and founder of a public company. He didn't talk about himself and his accomplishments. Instead, he was passionate about ideas and culture, and he was interested in my opinion.

He wasn't flirting, but he had this way of looking at me as though I was the only person in the room, and I found myself wanting to remember every word he said. I miss *that* Philip. I want to talk to him once more before he's gone.

CHAPTER TWENTY-TWO

FOR THE LAST THREE DAYS, PHILIP'S BEEN IN A MEDICALLY induced coma in a hospital in San Antonio. When the treatment was first explained to us, the idea sounded like something out of the Dark Ages: A chemotherapy so horrific, the only way his body could tolerate it was for him to be unconscious.

With each round of chemo, the three-day treatment marathon has grown exponentially more difficult for him. He struggles to do the things he used to take for granted like walking and eating, and I continue to second guess whether I've made the right decision. At least if he wasn't receiving chemotherapy, he might have a better quality of life.

I remind myself that every choice I make could mean life or death for him, and if I let it, the sheer weight of this responsibility will leave me babbling to myself in a dark corner. But it's in these moments, when I'm feeling overwhelmed, that I've learned to step out of his hospital room and walk down to the end of the hall and back.

Along the way, I pass dozens of rooms filled with other patients and their families who are facing similar challenges, and by the time I return to Philip's room, I realize we're all doing the best we can under an impossible situation. Sometimes I'm reminded that things aren't that different from our life before cancer. The one with the drug lab and the bodyguard. The situation then was grim, and I was waiting for something terrible to happen. I know how to do that except now, I'm the bodyguard.

During each three-day stretch he's unconscious, I keep detailed notes on every medication he's given and the time it's administered. I'm his private-duty nurse, which means I get little sleep, and it's a good thing I'm here. At the beginning of his second chemo marathon, I stopped a nurse from administering a second injection of the drug they used to put him to sleep.

"If you hadn't been paying attention," his oncologist told me, "it would've killed him on the spot."

Tonight I'm feeling especially alone and removed from the world. It's dark outside, and the only light in Philip's hospital room is coming from a television mounted on the wall. I've turned the volume down so low I can barely hear it. It's New Year's Eve, and in a few more minutes, it will be midnight.

The television cameras in Times Square are cutting back and forth from Dick Clark to closeups of the crowd. Couples and groups of people are bundled up in winter coats with scarves and hats to ward off the bitter cold. Some are kissing and drinking champagne while others are blowing kazoos and party horns in celebration of the impending new year. The only other sound in the room is the one the chemotherapy machine is making.

Be-dee be-deep. Be-dee be-deep. The sound means the chemo bag is empty. I push the call button and tell the nurse at the desk the bag needs to be replaced.

"It's a jubilant crowd of upwards of half a million people, and they're ready to bring in the New Year," Dick Clark says. "The temperature has dropped to 29 degrees, but this is the place to be on New Year's Rockin' Eve in New York City!"

The night nurse enters the room and begins hooking up a new bag of chemotherapy to Philip's IV. I double-check to make sure it's the right chemo and record the time in my notes.

The nurse looks down at Philip and then smiles at me. "I hope this next year will be a better one for both of you."

After she leaves the room, I turn off the overhead light and stand beside the head of his bed. In a soft voice I say, "I love you."

On television, the ball in Times Square is beginning to drop. The crowd is jubilant and they're singing, "We'll take a cup of kindness yet for days of auld lang syne."

I've always thought "Auld Lang Syne" was such a sad song, but this year, it's almost unbearable to hear. One of the few times I've allowed myself to cry was when Stephen and I were at the med school library. But now, the song and looking at Philip lying here, hooked up to IV bags and machines have stripped me of any sense of self-control, and I let the tears stream down my face.

I keep my voice low. "Just so you know, I don't like being the one in charge." I'm the person who's making life-and-death decisions that don't appear to be doing anything other than torturing him. Softly I stroke his forehead, careful not to do anything that will bring him out of his medically induced coma and make the effects of the chemotherapy worse than they already are.

He can't hear me, but out loud I whisper, "Have I failed you? Nothing I could have said in the last few years would have made any difference, would it?"

Outside the hospital window, San Antonio's skyline is lit up with colorful bursts of firework displays, but Philip and I have been exiled from the celebrations. We won't be a part of this happy new year, because, in my heart, I know this will be his last New Year's Eve.

CHAPTER TWENTY-THREE

I DON'T REMEMBER MUCH ABOUT MY FATHER'S CANCER except my mother and grandmother never talked about it unless I was out of the room. Other than having a nervous breakdown, like Mother did, I don't know how other families of terminal cancer patients get through this. Until their loved one takes their final breath, do they pray for a miracle and then wait, hoping for a life-saving reprieve? I'd like to know because I need all the help I can get, and whether he admits it or not, I suspect Philip needs even more.

Philip's a very private person, but on occasion, he's allowed me a glimpse into his deepest emotions. Like the day he found our cat, dead, on the side of the road. He'd picked him up and cradled him, and with tears in his eyes said, "Let's go home, buddy." That was the first time I'd ever seen him cry, and it moved me almost as much as the death of our favorite cat. Then there was the night his business partner died in a car accident. I found Philip outside in the hospital parking lot, crying. We'd embraced and stood with our arms around one another for a moment, then he'd pulled himself together and raised his "can't hurt steel" wall.

Now, when we're in the same room, we might as well be alone, because he doesn't want to have a conversation about anything. I feel as helpless as a tree stump, but I keep busy in the only way I know to help him: I've become a recognized member of his medical research team.

Regardless of whether he's in the hospital in San Antonio or at MD Anderson in Houston, if I ask the lab to draw three purple-topped tubes of Philip's blood, spin them down, label them, and give them to me, it happens without question, and my routine is always the same: I take the vials of his blood and drive to the nearest convenience store where I buy three Styrofoam coolers. Next, I drive to Baskin-Robbins and buy enough dry ice to fill all three. I pack one tube of his blood in a different cooler and then FedEx each one to a different cancer antigen researcher. The tests they run on his blood use cutting-edge technology, and we're hoping the results will track his body's response to the chemotherapy.

There are only a handful of researchers in the world who are working on cancer antigen markers, so there isn't a system in place to send them his blood. Philip's a scientist, and it feels only fitting that I've volunteered to be the middleman in this scientific effort. It's also something concrete I can do to keep myself from sinking further into depression. I have a purpose other than being his caregiver, chauffeur and bodyguard.

Two days after each shipment, I set my alarm for the middle of the night and call the researcher in Tokyo, then the one in Switzerland, and ask for the test results they've run on his blood. I'm hoping the different cancer antigen markers will have an affinity for his cancer and tell me if the chemotherapy is working.

With each call there's a language difficulty, and usually someone puts me on hold. Sometimes we lose the connection and I have to call them back. After each conversation, I take the results and plot the data on a graph I keep on a yellow legal pad. With each new mark on the graph, I hope for a downward trend of the markers which would mean the chemo is working, but other than a few temporary downward blips, the results offer nothing I can hold onto. Far from it. My middle-of-the-night phone calls plunge me further into a depression I hide from everyone.

The researchers are all interested in what I'm doing, and when I tell them I'm in communication with other cancer antigen researchers in different countries, they ask me to connect them with one another. I'm discovering new researchers every week, and since I'm the common denominator, Philip's oncologist at MD Anderson has suggested the possibility of hiring me to co-ordinate the same service for their other cancer patients. It's more than I can think about now because that would mean Philip is gone, and I'm not ready to deal with that yet.

CHAPTER TWENTY-FOUR

THE EARLY MORNING SUN IS PEEKING THROUGH THE gap between the drapes and the wall in our hotel room, and I'm barely awake when I hear Philip get out of bed. He can still make it on his own to the bathroom, but soon I may have to push him there in the wheelchair we sometimes use. The chemo has made his legs and feet feel heavy and numb like he's dragging around fifty-pound ankle weights, and it's getting harder for him to walk. He's a brave soldier, fighting an unwinnable war, but he hasn't complained or once questioned the choice of bullets.

I hear the bathroom door slam shut, followed by a loud thud. I scramble out of bed to the bathroom, but the door is blocked.

"Philip? Are you all right?" I manage to push the door open wide enough for me to slip inside. Philip is on the floor. "What happened?"

"I don't know. One moment I was fine and the next . . ."

"Did you hurt yourself?"

"I don't think so."

"Here. Take my arm." Philip is six foot three and 180 pounds. He's unsteady and a lot to handle alone, but I manage to get him on his feet.

"Just take me back to bed."

There are two beds in our hotel room. Both are hospital beds with controls that can raise and lower the head and feet. I lower his bed to make it easier for him to get in, but I can tell something's not right.

I make sure he's comfortable, and then call his doctor's nurse at the nearby National Cancer Institute in Bethesda, Maryland, and tell her what happened. I give her the facts, in order, everything I know so she can make an educated evaluation. I'm worried, but I don't want to say anything that will impair her judgment.

The nurse is familiar with our hotel on the edge of Washington, DC. It's where most of their outpatients and families stay when they're here for treatment. "He needs to be seen right away," she says. "An ambulance is on its way. I'll meet you in the hospital emergency room."

I'm in crisis mode which means I'll stay calm, not just with her, but no matter what happens. But this time, it's easier said than done. I force myself to table my emotions. *They'll cloud the issue and get in the way. Just breathe.*

I help Philip change from his pajama top into a shirt, but he shakes his head *no* when I ask if he'd like to put on a pair of slacks. I change into the same skirt and blouse I had on yesterday and run a toothbrush and a dab of paste across my teeth.

This week, Philip's been getting cutting-edge treatment, injections of monoclonal antibodies mixed with his cancer cells. His doctor, a world-renowned pioneer in the field of immunotherapy, hopes they'll act as little heat-seeking missiles with the ability to find Philip's cancer. If it works, perhaps they can administer targeted therapy to the cancer cells and leave the rest of his body alone. It occurs to me that something might have gone wrong with his injections, but I don't know enough to zero in on the problem.

In minutes there's a knock on the door of our hotel room, and four EMS technicians are standing in the hallway with a gurney. "We were driving past the hotel when we got the call," one of them says.

Two of the techs push past me, and in a well-coordinated move, they transfer Philip from the bed to the gurney. Another emergency technician is carrying what looks like an oversized fishing tackle box. He opens it, sets the top tray on the bed I've been sleeping in all week, and begins pulling things out of the box while a fourth technician with a clipboard starts asking me questions.

"Can you tell me what happened?"

The calm urgency in his voice doesn't escape me, but I force myself to focus on his questions.

"His name? Age? Is he taking any prescription meds?"

His questions are coming at a rapid-fire pace. I answer everything as concisely as I can while I watch the other emergency techs do their jobs. One of them has placed an oxygen mask over Philip's nose and mouth while another one is taking his blood pressure. A third one is inserting an IV into his arm. It's what I would expect them to do, but there's an accelerated seriousness to it all that scares me.

"What kind of treatment is he receiving?"

Before I can answer his question, Philip rips the oxygen mask away from his face and bolts upright on the gurney. His eyes are big, and he looks right at me. "I can't breathe!"

The man who's always calm in any situation is scared. I recognize his fear as the same one that's rising in my throat. I lean over and secure the mask back on his face.

"Darlin', you need to keep this on. It'll help you breathe." I make sure my voice is reassuring. "Everything's all right. You're going to be okay." I squeeze his hand and help him lie back down.

The urgency of the technicians' every move underscores the seriousness of what's happening, but I don't allow myself to think past letting them do their job and getting him to the hospital as fast as they can.

Two of the emergency techs have opened the door to our hotel room and have started rolling Philip's gurney down the hall toward the elevators. It's all happening so fast. I turn to grab my purse and notice the floor and both beds are littered with opened packets of alcohol wipes, rubber tourniquets, syringes, small glass vials, gauze, a roll of tape, and a pair of thin rubber gloves. It looks like a pharmaceutical supply store exploded in our room.

Once we're outside the hotel, the emergency techs open the rear doors of the ambulance and lift Philip and the gurney inside. When I try to get in with him, one of them tells me, "You need to ride up front."

I climb into the front passenger seat and the driver turns on the siren and pulls out of the hotel parking lot. As the ambulance races down the streets of Bethesda, the driver ignores the red and yellow streetlights, and the cars traveling in both directions pull over to let us pass. Every few seconds I turn and look over my shoulder through the cab's rear window, but I can't see him. He's hidden from view by the three emergency techs leaning over him. *They wouldn't all be clustered around him if something wasn't terribly wrong.*

The ambulance driver takes a hard left and comes to an abrupt stop in front of a hospital. He tells me to get out and wait inside the emergency room. The hospital's sliding glass doors open and two men, dressed in white, reach into the back of the ambulance to pull the gurney out.

I hear one of the techs inside the ambulance say, "If we move him, we'll lose him." Their words sear themselves across my heart.

My feet are bolted to the concrete near the rear of the ambulance. *I need to see him!* Someone takes me by the arm and pulls me out of the way, through the emergency room door, and into the hospital.

"The family waiting room's over there. The doctor will come to talk to you when he knows more."

Just as I've done for countless doctors' appointments, surgeries, chemotherapies, radiation treatments, and a bone marrow pull, I'm running on autopilot. No time for emotion or anything that will keep me and the doctors from making the best possible decisions. Like it's been so many times before, my world will be on hold until I know he's all right.

The next thing I know, Philip's nurse, the one I called from the hotel, is standing next to me. Philip's still in the back of the ambulance, but there are too many people in the way for us to see what's happening. In a few minutes, we see them lift the gurney out of the ambulance and roll it into the hospital. There's an emergency technician at either end, and four or five other people alongside, but I still can't see Philip. I haven't seen him since they lifted him into the ambulance. *I need to see his face. I need to know if he's conscious. If he looks like he's afraid.* In seconds, Philip and the medical convoy disappear through a set of swinging double doors.

Philip's nurse and I sit down on a small blue and green loveseat in the family waiting room. My voice is flat, void of all emotion, as I tell her everything that happened last night and this morning. What he had to eat, his routine since he saw the doctor, and how he had to cut the big thick book he'd been reading in half because his hands and arms weren't strong enough to hold the entire book. She's nodding at me, doing her best to be noncommittal.

Sitting here, waiting, is almost unbearable. No one's passed the open doorway of the little room we're in, not even an order-ly. The big hand on the round white wall clock continues to creep forward. Ten minutes, fifteen. My conversation with the nurse is killing time, talking about nothing that can help him.

It seems like we've been sitting here forever when a doctor appears in the doorway of the tiny waiting room.

"Mrs. Ray?"

I stand, and before he says anything else, I know this is one of those life-defining before-and-after moments.

"We lost him. I'm sorry."

Part of me wants to scream, "You haven't lost him! I watched you roll him down the hall. He's on the other side of those doors. Hurry! We need to find him!" But another part of me understands the words I've not let myself think about until now. Even when he was drinking and doing cocaine, on some level, I believed his silly statement, "You can't hurt steel." I thought—or maybe I hoped—I would get through to him, and he'd pull himself out of it, but Philip's stopped breathing. He's gone. Forever.

I no longer feel like I'm a part of the conversation with the doctor standing in front of me. It's as though someone else is having it, but I manage to ask, "What happened?"

"We're not sure, but with all the chemotherapy he's had, his veins were probably compromised. Was he taking a blood thin-ner?"

"No."

"Then it's possible he may have thrown a blood clot."

Philip's cancer nurse interrupts and puts her hand on my arm. "There's blood on the cushion where you've been sitting." She turns me around so I can see the sofa. Then she looks at what I'm wearing. "And you have blood on the back of your skirt."

I slide the waistband of my skirt around until I can see what she's talking about. A bright red bloom of blood has fanned out across the pale blue-and-white fabric like an abstract painting of a flower against the sky.

"It looks like you've started your period. We need to get you a tampon or something."

"But my last period ended a little over a week ago."

There's sadness and something that looks like pity in her eyes. "A sudden shock can do powerful things to our bodies."

I nod as though she's told me something trivial, but on some level, I already know this to be true. On the outside, I'm calm. My steely reserve is still a part of me, like a second layer of skin. I've lost all feeling and fear, and in their place is a detached numbness. The kind that comes from too much trauma. But inside, Philip's death has triggered an avalanche. A landslide of constant fear and years of barely hanging on is finally pouring out of me. I've controlled my feelings and pushed them down, and now, there's no more room for anything else.

CHAPTER TWENTY-FIVE

A WEEK AGO, I FLEW HOME FROM WASHINGTON, DC with Philip's body in a casket below me in the cargo hold. From my window seat, I watched the handoff from the funeral home to the baggage handlers as they lifted the lone transport funerary casket onto the moving ramp, and it disappeared into the belly of the plane. It was difficult to think about anything other than *I am taking my husband home in a box*. He was down there, alone in the dark, in between monogrammed golf bags and countless black zippered suitcases that all looked alike.

All the way home I imagined his body lying directly below me. He was still and expressionless, wearing the same shirt he left the hotel in, stretched out on a bed of white silk, his arms folded across his chest. His face was free of addiction, cancer, and pain. I wondered if he knew I was in the passenger seat above him, and what he might say to me if he could. The man who'd once thought with such laser focus now had the cloud of addiction lifted from his eyes and could see everything. Would he apologize, tell me he understood what he'd put me through, and help me understand the hell we'd both endured?

I wanted him to say he was sorry. I wanted to tell him I loved him, and I wished I could turn back the clock to the day he forgot to refill his Valium prescription. Like me, I wondered if he could trace the bodyguard at the door and the drug lab downstairs to that disastrous day. As much as I wanted to believe it hadn't changed him, I know it did. He must have known it too.

A dozen times during the flight I teared up, and each time I stopped myself from disintegrating into heaving sobs because I knew they would turn into howls and mournful cries, and it wasn't time to let that part of me out. Not until I was alone. For years, I've thrown up brick walls to keep from feeling the nightmare that was more than cancer. I've grieved the death of self and dignity, both his and mine, and it will take more than tears and howling at the moon to make things right again.

It's strange how you can wake up one morning, and ten seconds later life as you know it has ended. One moment I was beginning a new day and an hour later, my husband was dead. This is not how I saw it ending. *This is not what I wanted for you, Philip. Not what I wanted for us. You were a good man who was blinded by addiction. You boarded the wrong train.*

My thoughts drift back to the hotel room that morning. *Did I make light of your fears when I knelt and put the oxygen mask back on your face and said, "It'll help you breathe"? When they loaded you into the ambulance, should I have ignored the emergency techs and bent down and put my head next to yours on the gurney, and held your hand on the way to the hospital? I should have been there, next to you, as your life was slipping away. You needed to know you were loved. That I was there, still fighting for you.*

Did you know you were going to die? Did you fear death? I have so many questions that will go unanswered. At least if I knew what you were thinking, maybe I could begin to process things better.

Grief is love and great loss with no place to go, but it doesn't feel the way I thought it would. It's not a one-size-fits-all process. I haven't been paralyzed and taken to my knees like my mother was after my father died. The grief I feel now is for what his addiction did to us, the dark places it subjected us to, and the fear that neither one of us would find our way out.

Some days are harder than others, but I'm still making phone calls and arrangements, going through the motions of what needs to be done. When the shock wears off, perhaps extreme anguish and bereavement will engulf me like a shroud, but for now, my tears are more for the tall, gorgeous guy. The one who took my breath away. The handsome, luminous man who loved life and loved me and taught me so many amazing things. I will always miss that man, but he died from the effects of drugs and alcohol, and I grieved for him a long time ago.

This morning I called a woman I know, a woman much older than I am, whose husband died after years of a prolonged illness. When I asked how she was doing, she'd replied, "I'm going to be candid with you. I'm relieved."

It's as though her words were intended just for me. I wanted to tell her I understood what she was saying. It doesn't mean she didn't love her husband and wasn't grieving for him, only that she's relieved it's over. For both of them. I wonder if she tells this to other people, will they find her truthful admission shocking and inappropriate? And if they do, perhaps it's because they—or a loved one—haven't gone through anything so debilitating and demeaning, or maybe they're not being honest with themselves.

There may be those who would judge me if I told them I felt the same way. Right now people are offering me their sympathy, but what they don't know is that I'm not grieving like they think I should. Like the woman I called this morning, I'm relieved. For both of us.

For Philip, his brutal battle with himself is over, and the

painful rigors of cancer treatment have stopped, but I'm just beginning to realize how long I've kept years of nonstop fear bottled up inside me. How I've kept Guido and Little Louie and everything that's spiraled out of control walled off, waiting just below the surface to break free. Sometimes I managed to act as though nothing bad would come from any of it. Other times it kept me awake at night, recalling the subtleties of how I let myself be roped in, again and again, hoping he would change, only for him to rear up and lunge at me like a wild animal.

I was the woman who lived with the cocaine craziness and the smokeless cigarette threats. The same woman who did normal things like go to the grocery store and take my dog to the vet. *I'm fine, thank you. Yes, have a good day.* Separating the two was the only way I could get up and fight my way through another day. The only way I could put on my *everything's okay* mask and pretend to the outside world it was true. That life didn't seem so distorted and depraved.

Even our closest friends don't know how difficult the last seven or eight years have been, not just since he was diagnosed with terminal cancer a year ago. They don't know about the times I ran from the house in fear. The times I wondered if the next morning he would be the Philip I once knew, or if he would remain the same dark and troubled soul who didn't care about himself, much less me.

Philip, your death has taken me by surprise. I never saw it happening this way, but I'm grateful it wasn't prolonged and painful where you withered and grew weak mentally as well as physically. Not being there mentally would have been harder for you than dying, but then maybe that's why you chose to self-medicate with cocaine and alcohol. After the Valium, you knew you were a different man.

I can't stop wondering if I should've insisted we talk about dying—about your fears and mine. You made it clear it wasn't a conversation you wanted to have, but it would've helped me, and in the end, it might have helped you as well. Or were you afraid to let me see the anguish you felt and perhaps the regret? If you had it all to do over, would you have done things differently? I'd like to believe you wouldn't have started the project in the lab, and I would've put up more of a fight to stop you.

I loved you more than I loved myself. Then again, maybe I feared losing you if your train moved on without me because I'd lost all sense of self-awareness and what was good for me. Like the job you had in high school painting window signs for grocery stores that said "Sale" or "Green Beans $.39 a Pound," did you paint an imaginary S on my forehead? "Stupid, naïve young woman who will do anything you want her to do."

With one hand I struggled to hang on to your high-speed train, and with the other I tried to protect you, hoping things would return to the way they used to be. But part of me wonders if you used me. That's not how you treat someone you love, and I don't want to believe that because then I will hate you.

I don't want to feel this anger and disappointment forever because I loved and adored you. Did you know that? Damn you! Did you know that? Did it mean anything to you, or were you counting on that? I want to remember you as charismatic and spellbinding instead of beating myself up because nothing I could have done would have changed a thing. Addicts don't want to let go of their addiction.

This is the clearest I've let myself think and feel since Philip built the lab downstairs. *Where have I been all this time, and how will I learn to breathe again? How will I let go of my fears about what was happening in the lab and whether you would hurt yourself or me? I want to know what it feels like to* breathe in simple things like sunrises and sunsets and savor them while they nurture my spirit. I don't remember the last time I took a breath like that. The last time I didn't need to be afraid of monsters under the bed—or the person lying next to me.

I'm not sure I know who I am on my own, and when I start breathing, whose breath will I be inhaling? How will I redefine myself and find my new normal? It scares me to wonder who I might've been if I'd put the same energy into myself as I did into being your everything. If I hadn't turned my back on who I was and what I needed.

I will take your life lessons and remember the good things. I'll forgive you for your trespasses as I hope you'll forgive me for mine. I love you, Philip, but damn you! How long am I going to keep saying, "Damn you"?

CHAPTER TWENTY-SIX

"YOU CAN ALWAYS LIVE IN MOTHER'S LITTLE HOUSE," HE'D told me, a reference to the small two-bedroom, one-bath red brick house in the country he bought for his mother.

I remember the way the low afternoon sun glinted off the face of his watch and how the Movado's trademark gold dot was reflected onto the ceiling. How it hovered and danced as though it hung on his every word, like I did. The way he sat in his usual corner of the sofa, looking out over the city, and how he'd chosen not to look at me when he spoke.

It was one of those moments I should've stopped and asked what he meant, but he was bald and sick from chemo and having trouble walking. He had enough to handle without me bringing something up that could have added to his burdens.

Now I know everything Philip knew that day: In six months, the balloon note on our home will be due. After seventeen years together we owe three years' back taxes, penalties, and interest, and we have colossal credit card debt and over a million dollars' worth of cancer bills. On the other side of the ledger, there's no money in the bank. No life insurance or death benefit on the mortgage. No more Datapoint stock. Nothing except a lot of Advanced Tobacco smokeless cigarette stock which may never be good for anything other than wallpapering the bathroom. At least there's still a small investment portfolio with a brokerage firm downtown.

Why didn't you tell me what you meant about living in Mother's little house? Or maybe I should be blaming myself for not asking.

Today's mail is full of more cancer bills, and I've put them on the dining room table along with dozens of other cancer bills I've opened and noted in the spreadsheet I've made: lung biopsy, lung surgery; dozens of lab tests in three cities; eight three-day hospital stays of coma-induced chemotherapy, ten radiation treatments, a bone marrow pull, monoclonal antibody injections, MRIs and X-rays; oncologists in San Antonio, more doctors at MD Anderson in Houston and the National Cancer Institute; the EMS in Bethesda, and the emergency room where he died; an autopsy and air transport to bring his body home; embalming, a memorial service, a cemetery plot, and burial.

I've checked every line item and circled the questionable ones, like the $30 Band-Aids and $1,000 bags of chemotherapy he never received. Like the Maya who buried their dead with a jade bead in their mouth as safe passage to the next life, I don't have the money to pay for anyone else's jade beads—except Philip's—and I paid for it with an emerald.

At the funeral home the night before he was buried, I had a family member put Philip's emerald in the breast pocket of his suit. I've always referred to it as "Philip's emerald" because he didn't buy it for me. He bought it for the little boy who grew up in the tin shack with the dirt floor, and I wanted to send that little boy on his way with his emerald. A gesture I now realize was nothing more than a bunch of romanticized nonsense.

Perhaps I was tired and overwhelmed and not thinking straight. Or maybe, like the Egyptians who believed emeralds were a sign of rebirth, it was my way of hoping Philip would find himself again. Either way, he disappeared into the ground with a flawless one-carat emerald he didn't need. A stone that could've helped me pay a mountain of bills I knew nothing about. Now I'm selling cars and furniture and things out of my house just to keep the lights on, food in the refrigerator, and pay the property taxes. I traded one of Philip's guns to my hairstylist in exchange for a year's worth of color and cuts and another one to the electrician who replaced the old, antiquated fuse box in the kitchen.

On more than one occasion I can remember Philip saying he wanted "to run out of money and breath at the same time. Anything after that and I will have lost interest." Each time I'd laughed because it had a certain morose humor to it, but now I think he meant it.

Another time he said, "Insurance is a sucker's bet. I'd rather take the money I would spend on insurance policies and bet it on myself. And I'm betting I can create a better return on my investment than the money an insurance policy would leave you."

That was easy for him to say. The Philip who made that statement didn't drink or do drugs, but that's not the Philip who left me here, alone, to face the IRS and the mortgage company with less than enough money to appease them both. The man who'd announced I could live in Mother's little house had known this day was coming. He took the chickenshit way out, and I'm this side of despising him for it.

For the last hour, all I've done is stare at the spreadsheet and wonder which things need to be paid off first and which ones can be paid in monthly installments. Isn't it ironic? I'm the one who's in control of the checkbook now. The person who, for the last seventeen years, received a $500 monthly allowance while Philip was free to buy a new Porsche whenever he wanted and build a chemistry lab. I may not have participated in the decisions on how to manage *our* money, but I handled the accounts payable for a public company. I understand the most fundamental rule of accounting: Don't let the amount of cash going out exceed the amount of cash coming in.

Other than clothes for a special occasion, the only time I asked for something that cost more than my allowance was when I wanted a better camera. He bought me a used Pentax for my college photography class, and I took it everywhere. It became an extension of me, but as I started using my journalism and photography skills professionally, I'd asked for a better camera with at least one good lens. He bought them for me, but not before he asked, "Is this a need or a want?"

Whenever he posed that question—the camera wasn't the only time—I realized it was coming from the little boy who'd grown up with nothing and now could buy whatever he wanted. The little boy for whom the rules of need and want no longer applied. While Philip's the one who got us into this precarious financial mess I knew nothing about, he may have done me a favor, because I've created a new accounting rule for myself: *If I can't pay cash for something, I don't need it.* While it's a good idea, my new fiscal rule will have to wait until I figure out how to deal with the pile of debt I've inherited.

The afternoon sun has washed the walls of the home I may not be able to keep with warm rays of honey and gold, and it's colored the shadows a soft earthy brown. In contrast, I think about the place across the freeway where the homeless people gather to panhandle at the stoplight on the access road, and I'm reminded there's a very real chance I could wind up living in a cardboard box under a bridge somewhere.

There are a half-dozen big financial dilemmas in front of me, but I need more information before I can decide what to do about any of them. At this point I'm not sure I even know the right questions to ask, or whom to ask. Except for a few friends,

I don't feel safe sharing the details of my life, but even with them, I'm too embarrassed to lay out the wreckage of our finances.

I turn on the lights in Philip's dressing room and start opening his dresser drawers. I pull out socks and underwear, a lint roller, a pocketknife, and restaurant matchbooks. In the bottom drawer, I find his handwritten notes for the first draft of Advanced Tobacco Products' business plan. Nothing I find is helpful. Nothing gives me clarity about the next steps I need to take.

On the top shelf of his closet there's a stack of papers, and on the bottom are some of our tax returns. Once again I'm reminded that *ours* isn't a word either one of us would have applied to money and yet, *I'm* the one who's liable for *our* debts. Like everything else about the newly discovered information on our finances, I've put a lid on my anger. It's not helpful, but more than that, I can't let anger define me.

Paper-clipped to one of the tax returns is a business card with the phone number of Philip's accountant. I dial the number and begin asking him about the three years of back taxes, penalty, and interest.

"It all comes as a surprise, and I'd appreciate it if you could help me understand how this happened. How much do I owe the IRS, and how long do I have to pay them?"

"Every year you signed those tax returns," he replies. "Now you tell me you didn't know what you were signing?" The tone in his voice denotes more than a hint of skepticism. "Why would you sign something you didn't understand?" Before I can answer he adds, "Surely you don't believe I can make this all go away." The snort he makes at the end of his sentence makes it clear he thinks I'm a bimbo.

Hasn't he been listening to anything I've said? I never asked him to make it go away. *Why is this so difficult to understand?* I trusted my husband to do the right thing. I was seldom involved in the financial side of the investments he made, and I didn't know anything about the taxes we owed—or the balloon note due on our house. We never talked about taxes except when it came time for him to put the completed annual tax form in front of me to sign. I always *assumed* everything was in order—all the gains and losses, and the line items like depreciation were as they should be. I can't be the first wife who's found herself in this position, but I get the message. Shame on me. It's a mistake I'll never make again, but right now, I need some advice. I need to know my options.

I hang up and make an appointment with the tax attorney at Advanced Tobacco Products' law firm. The same attorney who wrote our wills when everyone thought we were destined to become smokeless cigarette billionaires.

Like Philip's accountant, the next day in his downtown office the lawyer is less than forthcoming with information. Instead he stands there, staring at me with a look of disdain.

"I take it you've read the will." His voice is condescending as he nods at the copy I've brought with me. "You were there when the three of us talked about it. You signed it. Everything you need to know is in the will."

Is there no one I can go to for advice? I want to ask if he treats every shell-shocked and grieving widow this way. Instead I say, "Philip's mother needs to be taken care of, the payments on the house he bought her need to be made, and I have a long list of other debts. I'm hoping you can help me prioritize them. Other than his mother, should the IRS come before the rest of our bills?"

"As executor of your husband's estate, you can do whatever you want."

There's that word again. *Want.* The yin to the yang of *need*. After thirty minutes of finding different ways to ask the same question, it becomes clear that *you can do whatever you want* is the only answer he's going to give me. His silence might as well be highlighted in bold jerk-weed neon.

Philip's legal business has made this law firm and its partners a bucketload of money. They own a significant piece of Advanced Tobacco stock and probably Datapoint stock as well, not to mention they were the law firm for another one of Philip's startups and several other high-tech Datapoint spinoffs. I thought they'd be only too happy to advise me, but here I sit, dumbfounded by their lack of interest.

I'm out here, all by myself, crouched on a narrow fiscal ledge, and for the first time since Philip's death, I feel the full weight of being alone. I'm like a butterfly that's partially emerged from its chrysalis, and the most vulnerable parts of my new life are exposed and unfamiliar, especially to me. Instead of a big, cozy oak tree in my backyard, my uncharted place of emergence is on the twenty-third floor of the law firm's building.

An unnerving thought makes me wrap my newfound wings around my body. What if the law firm's partners know about Philip's lab and his cocaine-and-alcohol-fueled craziness? What if they see me as a coconspirator and their pedigreed firm wants nothing to do with me? Unless the tax attorney is a total asshole, and I haven't ruled that out, what other reason would he have for standing at the far end of the conference table and staring at me with such a look of contempt?

Like a butterfly when it breaks free of its casing, I'm a new creature in an unexplored world, and regardless of whether I succeed or fail, I've learned another important rule: Never trust anyone whose eyes don't match the look on their face because a phony smile and a look of contempt don't go together.

CHAPTER TWENTY-SEVEN

I'M THIRTY-EIGHT, FIVE YEARS OLDER THAN PHILIP WAS when we first started seeing one another seventeen years ago. Half of our years together were happy, but the rest were spent dodging grenades he hurled at me from the dungeon. I'm not the same woman I was at twenty-one. I'm not as trusting, and just as I have a PhD in trauma, I've earned one in addiction and drug-induced crazy.

Mentally, physically, and emotionally I'm exhausted, and on the nights I have trouble sleeping, I lie in bed and replay the same broken record. I know all the lyrics by heart, and each stanza starts with love and ends with cocaine, alcohol, and cancer.

Some nights I wonder what went through his mind at the end. If he thought about his legacy or if his conscience bothered him the least little bit? Sometimes he made me feel like I was the center of his universe, but what if I was merely the audience for his? Other nights I half-expect to see him coming up the stairs from the dungeon, and I find myself tensing up, waiting for him to detonate the next crisis. But most nights it's hard for me to concentrate on television, and my short attention span can't handle a book. Right now magazines are more my speed. I can look at the pictures and scan the captions, knowing I'll forget them as soon as I turn the page, and that's okay. Magazines are short-term diversions with no beginning and no end, and no plot to string together from page to page.

Earlier this evening, I disconnected the plastic Radio Shack intercom that kept me connected to the lab and I put it in the trash next to an empty box of macaroni and cheese. Like the empty carton, part of me is hollow and vacant while the other part doesn't know what to do with all my questions. I keep thinking he didn't care enough to tell me about our finances and the balloon note due on the house. If he told me, maybe I wouldn't feel so hurt.

Phydaux has jumped up next to me on the sofa. His big brown eyes are sad and worried.

"It's okay, sweet boy." My voice is soft, and I rub his ears and the top of his head. "We're going to be all right. I promise."

He lies down with his head on his paws, but his eyes keep darting back and forth from my face to a random spot on the wall. He's waiting for me to relax so he doesn't have to worry about me. My hand moves from his head, down his back to his tail, and he lets out a heavy sigh and closes his eyes. I take it as a sign I need to do the same. If only I knew how.

Outside on the freeway life goes on, and tonight is like most of the other six thousand some-odd nights I've sat here, looking out over the city. It's the same scene I would've seen two months ago or seventeen years ago. The headlights and taillights still twinkle and shimmer and silently disappear over the horizon. Blinking red lights still magically glide across the sky and descend to their designated landing strip in the middle of the city. Out there nothing has changed, but in here I swing back and forth between being sad and depressed to the realization I've been this way for years.

I've called a scientist friend and asked him to help me clean out Philip's lab. I don't know if he's aware of what he's removing, but he's careful not to spill the heavy beakers of mercury or touch the crystalline substances growing on some of the metal surfaces. I have him take the refrigerator and its contents, the Erlenmeyer flasks, the Corning Ware, the glass rods, and the swivel chair. I don't want to see any of it ever again.

Except for the ragged blue carpeting and the overhead vent hood, the contents of the room are gone. On the top of Philip's worktable are notations he's written in pencil. Chemical formulas, mathematical equations, and a phone number I don't recognize. Even if the room was gutted and repainted and I installed new carpeting, I won't be able to forget what happened here. How it bubbled up and blanketed everything. How it destroyed our lives.

There's an open bottle of chardonnay in my hand. It's been a long time since I felt safe enough to let my guard down and have a drink of anything. Not during cocaine or chemotherapy, but if I had to guess, I'd say the bottle will be empty by the end of the night.

I've gathered all of Philip's notes and his papers about the recipe, and I'm burning them in a pit in the side yard where an ornate Mexican-tiled fountain once stood. I take another swallow of wine and watch the burning embers drift skyward, an everchanging architectural flurry of fireflies that drift and pop and die on the wind. My own private fireworks display with the city lights as the backdrop.

Philip's work has gone up in smoke, and I couldn't recreate

his list of reference books if my life depended on it. Should Guido and Little Louie come for me, they need to know there's nothing left to take but my soul and my tenacity. They should also know I will never go quietly or willingly for anyone ever again.

The fire in the pit has died down, and years of lost and misplaced dreams have turned to ash. I'm reminded of the Mexican *bruja* and the burning ceremony she conducted before my abortion. I was seventeen. She'd muttered and whispered to herself as she waved a bundle of smoking, strange-smelling sticks around the tiny motel room as though she was erasing words and images from an unseen blackboard.

Now I know it was sage the *bruja* burned that day, and tomorrow I will buy a bundle of the same dried sticks tied together with string. I will open all the doors and windows, every dresser drawer and closet and cupboard full of dishes. I will light the ends and cleanse away the Nazi spies and the bad karma left by Dr. Jekyll and Mr. Hyde. I will release the Spy House on the Hill, and myself, from every invisible force of dark energy and banish everything that has no place in my future.

CHAPTER TWENTY-EIGHT

EVEN WITH ALL THE VIOLENCE AND THE INSANITY THAT'S taken place inside these storied walls—before and after we moved in—I love my home. I can't imagine living anywhere else. But what if I can't pay off the balloon note before it's due? What if the IRS takes my house as a down payment on what I owe them?

The house and the land it sits on are high above the freeway on the corner of one of the busiest intersections in town. Someday it will be more valuable than everything else I have put together, and it's occurred to me that if the house was paid for, the IRS couldn't take it away from me. I know that much without getting any more bad-mannered expert advice.

I reach for the coupon book from the savings and loan company. Inside, each stub lists the monthly payments and breaks them down into principal and interest owed, and the total amount due. Printed on the front of the book is the company's Houston address and phone number.

I call the number, and the operator transfers me to a loan officer named Ken. I give him my name and the loan number and explain my predicament: I don't have enough money to pay off the mortgage and the rest of my bills, and the $79,000 balloon note is due on May first, eight months from now.

"No problem," Ken says. "We'll just restructure your loan to a thirty-year payout."

While he's telling me what the savings and loan company will need in order to issue me a new loan, I feel myself choking up with emotion. It's a good thing Ken is a talker because I don't want to break down in tears over the phone.

"Thank you," I manage to say. "I can't tell you how grateful I am."

I won't have to come up with the entire amount due on the house, and I can use what's in Philip's stock portfolio to take care of his mother and begin to pay down the rest of my debts. I hang up and give in to my tears. I've been doing a lot of that lately, but this time they're a mixture of stress and the hope that I've taken a viable first step to get myself out of my financial bind.

CHAPTER TWENTY-NINE

FOR THE LAST THREE MONTHS, THE SAVINGS AND LOAN company in Houston has taken the lead in a deceptive dance they've been doing with me. At the beginning of each month I call Ken, who continues to assure me they will restructure my loan. "We'll start it on the first of next month." But when the first rolls around, Ken has a ready excuse for why it's been postponed, again.

"We've decided it would be better if we restructured your loan to begin on the first of the year." At the time it sounded reasonable. Lots of things have start dates of January 1, but when January 1 arrived, and then February 1, Ken had other excuses. One month he wanted the letters testamentary, and Philip's signed will that made me executor of his estate.

"But I sent you those three months ago."

"Did you? I'm sure they're here somewhere. Just to be sure, why don't you send them to me again."

When I call him on March 1, Ken begins with an apology. "Several things have taken precedence over your loan, but don't worry. We'll make it happen."

"My balloon note comes due May 1," I remind him.

"We have plenty of time. We'll get it done."

April 1 comes, and Ken says he's getting my paperwork

together, and he'll call me next week but when next week arrives, I don't hear from him, and he doesn't return my calls. Something's not right. I can feel it, and I've started calling him twice a day. It's the third week in April, a little over a week until my balloon note is due before Ken takes my call.

"Mrs. Ray, we're unable to issue you a new loan."

"But since the beginning of September, you've assured me it was all but a done deal. You just had to dot the i's and cross the t's."

"When we reviewed your application for a new loan, we noticed you don't have a full-time job. It's not our policy to issue a loan to someone who doesn't have a steady income."

Something smells bad, and it's not my lack of what he considers a full-time job. Like the tax attorney at the law firm, I have a feeling Ken's eyes don't match the rest of his face.

"When we first started talking in September, you knew my income came from writing business plans for entrepreneurs, and you had no problem with that. All these months, you've been leading me on, haven't you?" I pause and give Ken the opportunity to answer my accusation, but he says nothing. I proceed to list all the excuses he's given me over the last seven months. "Now I'm down to the wire, and you tell me what you've known all along. You're trying to take my house, aren't you, Ken?"

Once again, my comments are met with silence.

"If you were on the level, you would have told me this months ago. Is this how you want someone to treat your wife or your mother? To steal their home out from under them?"

"I would never leave my wife or my mother in such a vulnerable position."

He's all but admitted this is what the savings and loan company has been doing.

I remember a recent *Wall Street Journal* article about the

S&L crisis, and if I recall correctly, I'm not the only one whose home is being taken by the savings and loan companies. I want to tell Ken what a lowlife snake in the grass he is, but instead, I hang up. I've already been taken advantage of by someone I loved, and I'm not going to let some glass and steel corporation filled with faceless scumbags take my home.

Ken doesn't know it, but he's made my decision for me, and I have only a few days to carry out my plan. The first rule I made after Philip's death may have been more prophetic than I imagined: If I can't pay cash for something, I don't need it.

I call the stockbroker and ask how much is left in Philip's investment account. There's just enough to pay off the note. Without hesitating, I tell him to liquidate enough to cover the balloon note on my house.

"But that's almost everything you have," he says.

"I know, and I need you to do it, immediately. Please make the check payable to me, executor of Philip's estate." I plan to leave a clear paper trail of everything I'm doing. "And just so we're on the same page, I need the check no later than the day after tomorrow." I have until the beginning of next week, but he doesn't need to know that. I'm not taking any chances.

I'm known for being easygoing and considering what I've been through, I've handled myself with remarkable and uncommon grace, but now I'm pissed off! Ken and his savings and loan company can go fuck themselves! This is *my* house, and no one's going to swindle me out of it.

Houston is a three-and-a-half-hour drive from San Antonio, and I leave the house at six-thirty in the morning. Plenty of time to get there before the crazy afternoon rush hour on the Houston freeways.

When I get to Houston, I exit Highway 610 and turn right on Post Oak Boulevard. I find the savings and loan company and pull into their parking lot. Just as I thought. The building is made of steel and glass. There's a receptionist at a desk in the lobby, and I ask her to direct me to Ken Strickland's office.

"Is he expecting you?"

"No, he's not." But to myself, I think, *If he has half a brain he shouldn't be surprised.*

Ten minutes go by before a soft doughy man in a nondescript grey suit exits the elevator. He stops at the receptionist's desk, and she makes a motion with her head to where I'm sitting.

Ken Strickland is clearly flustered. He approaches me and makes an awkward attempt to extend his hand.

I stand but I don't offer my hand in return. "I'm here to pay off my loan. The one that's due next week." Ken's face has lost all color, and he's staring at me like I'm an apparition. "Is there somewhere we can go to take care of the paperwork?"

Ken wasn't prepared for me to be standing in front of him with Philip's signed and notarized will, the letters of testamentary, designating me as the person with the ability to act on behalf of his estate, and a cashier's check made out to the savings and loan company for the exact amount of the balloon note due on my home. In addition, I've brought my checkbook in case the final amount is more than Ken calculated. Part of me wants to say *checkmate asshole*, but as usual, I bite my tongue.

After the paperwork is done and the house is mine, I sit outside in my car and cry, not for how close I came to losing my home, but how close I came to losing myself. In the past, sometimes I pretended to be brave to impress Philip, but with this move, I've built a bridge back to myself. Back to the strong woman I've always been. I'm gutsy and brave, and this has been the next step in reclaiming my power.

I think about the little girl with asthma who watched through the front window of my parents' living room as the neighborhood kids built a snowman outside. I can build my own snowman, and I don't need anyone's help. This experience has taught me a lot about myself and life after Philip. I'm doing fine on my own, and it feels good to be in control. I vow to remember this if life leads me astray again.

The Spy House on the Hill, @1980, San Antonio, Texas.
Photo by Brenda Ray Coffee.

Jon Philip Ray, @1971, CEO/Founder of Datapoint Corporation;
inventor of the Datapoint 3300, the first desktop computer terminal;
the Datapoint 2200, the first personal computer, and the microprocessor.
He was also CEO/Founder of Advanced Tobacco Products,
and inventor of FAVOR® the first smokeless cigarette.
Photo from the Archives of Jon Philip Ray.

Philip Ray and Brenda Ray Coffee, @1972, San Antonio, Texas.
Photo from the Archives of Jon Philip Ray.

Brenda Ray Coffee, @1973, The Bahamas. Photo by Philip Ray.

Brenda Ray Coffee, self-portrait, @1978,
the red barn behind the Spy House on the Hill.

The IEEE Region 5 Stepping Stone Award

for the

Datapoint 2200 Desktop Personal Computer

AS THE FIRST PERSONAL COMPUTER

The San Antonio Museum of
Sciences and Technology
102 Mabry Dr.
Port San Antonio
San Antonio, TX 78226

May 28th, 2022,
11:00 am – 12:30 pm
Reception to follow

Program from the 2022 official ceremony designating the Datapoint
2200 as the "First Personal Computer."

Brenda Ray Coffee, 1982, in Air Force fighter jet for *Southwest Airlines Magazine* article, "30 Seconds Over Hondo." Photo by Rob Beach.

Comedor & Hospedaje Brenda, 1988, Tikal, Guatemala.
Photo by Brenda Ray Coffee.

FAVOR® Smokeless Cigarettes, the first vape, @1985, invented by Jon Philip Ray. Brenda Ray Coffee named it FAVOR® and was the first to coin the terms *vape* and *vaping*. Photo by Brenda Ray Coffee.

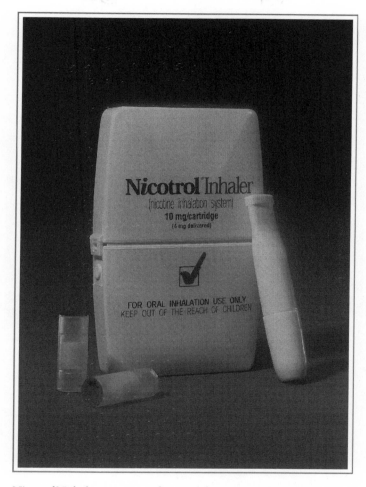

Nicotrol® Inhaler, @1998, redesigned from Jon Philip Ray's original smokeless cigarette patent which Advanced Tobacco Products' board of directors sold to Pharmacia & Upjohn, where it joined the Nicorette®/Nicotrol® Patch, Gum, and Nasal Spray.
Photo Advanced Tobacco Products.

Brenda Ray Coffee and James Coffee at their wedding reception, 1996.
Photo by Melanie Rush Davis.

PART TWO

GUATEMALA

"It is impossible for you to go on as you were before,
so you must go on as you never have."

—CHERYL STRAYED

CHAPTER THIRTY

EACH NIGHT FOR THE LAST WEEK THE WAVES HAVE LULLED me to sleep like the beats of a mother's heart, and the healing power of the saltwater has kissed away the cuts and scrapes I've gotten while snorkeling off the island of Ambergris Caye in Belize. There's something soothing and mesmerizing about the colors and sounds of the ocean, and they speak to me on a primal level as though I emerged from the sea instead of from my mother's womb.

Like the bills I've paid, I've sold things out of my house to pay for this trip. Pretty gewgaws that sit on end tables and hang on walls. I'm grateful I still have my house and things to sell because my health and well-being have become my top priority, and this trip has been a much-needed break.

It's been a long time since I haven't had any worries, and my time here has been restorative. It's helped me recapture parts of myself that died or were lost in the cocaine and cancer madness. In many ways, it's helped that I rented one of the thatched cabanas on the beach where Philip and I stayed some years ago when we were here with friends. I think that's why I came here. To help me let go of everything that's happened and to remind me of the good times when everything was right with my world.

I've been reminded of how Philip would sometimes hold my

hand when we snorkeled or went scuba diving. How he taught me what to look for like the stingray that buried itself in the sand, or the octopus that changed its appearance from smooth to mottled and bumpy and then folded in on itself and disappeared in a blink. On my own I would have zoomed right past them, but he taught me how to be thoughtful and take my time.

This week I've delighted in the delicate red and white peppermint-striped shrimp that cling to the seagrass. Next to them a group of tiny fish dodged and weaved through hidden passageways in the coral and emerged through another opening no bigger than a minute. So many magnificent and mysterious creatures, a world where I'm the alien, the one who is trespassing in their unique and uncommon universe.

I've left Ambergris Caye, and I'm high above the ocean, the only passenger in a small puddle jumper. Its shadow on the water below looks like a tiny toy plane, sailing effortlessly across the sea, and the colors of the ocean make me think of my young friend, Tory, and her big box of crayons. We both liked the blue one named "Tulum." No one can appreciate why a color would be named after an ancient Maya ruin unless they've climbed to the top of Tulum's Temple of the Wind God and gazed out over the sea. Tulum's not the largest or most spectacular Maya ruin, but it's my favorite, and the ocean below me is washed in shades of robin's egg blue, turquoise, peacock, and Tulum.

The pilot calls to me over his shoulder. "Better buckle up! We'll be landing in a few minutes."

He's a Humphrey Bogart *To Have and Have Not* kind of guy, and he's wearing a navy nautical cap with a black visor and blue jeans. Somewhere in his past, I'm betting his story was derailed by wine, women, and a jealous husband.

The dark, vibrant blues of the ocean have faded into paler and paler shades of aquamarine—a sure sign the water's getting shallower and the mainland of Belize isn't far. I'm excited to land and get on with the rest of my journey. A few days ago on Ambergris Caye, I met Hilde and Carson, a delightful British couple, and we decided to visit the Maya ruin of Tikal in Guatemala, the country to the west of Belize. The three of us liked ancient archaeological sites, but when Carson couldn't change their return reservations to London, I decided to go alone.

This won't be the first time I've been to a Maya ruin alone. I've lost track of how many times Philip and I went to the Yucatán, and while everyone else took an afternoon nap, I would drive the rental Jeep to Tulum. This time I don't have a Jeep, but I've been told I can catch a bus in Belize City that will take me to Tikal, and that's fine with me because it's been a long time since I've had an adventure.

The pilot lines the small plane up with the end of the runway. The wheels touch down, and he taxis up to a small cinder block building. When the propeller blades stop spinning, he helps me out and hands me my bags.

"Except for a guy in the air traffic control tower, the airport's closed today," he says, "but someone outside on the street can tell you where to catch the bus to Tikal." He waves and says, "Good luck!"

The people who owned the cabanas on Ambergris Caye didn't say anything about the airport being closed. In fact, they told me while I was here I could change my return flight home on TACA—nicknamed Take a Chance Airways, the unreliable and sometimes scary airline that services Belize—to another flight leaving out of Guatemala City. And like the bus that will take me to Tikal, I can catch another bus there that will take me to the airport in Guatemala City. I'm not crazy about being without a reservation, but if I want to see Tikal, it's my only option.

On the street outside the airport, Belize City stands in stark contrast to the beautiful island paradise of Ambergris Caye. The first thing I notice is an open market that runs alongside a garbage-strewn canal. Even from here, it smells like feces and overripe bananas, and the water in the canal is a rusty red, with lambs and children crossing in the middle.

I'm surprised I haven't seen a taxi. I've traveled a lot in Mexico and taxis are easy to find there, especially in a coastal town the size of Belize City. On the other hand, except for a handful of tourists, I don't imagine the locals at the market can afford a taxi.

There's a policeman on the corner who tells me, "If it's running today, there's a bus to Tikal," but first I must find a pharmacy a few blocks down and to the right called Li Ho. "Look for a sign with a skull and crossbones hanging over the door. They're licensed to sell drugs and poison. Ask for a Jamaican, named Taj, who can drive you to the bus stop."

As I turn to leave, the policeman says, "Taj is always high on ganja. He'll try and hustle you about one thing or another all the way to the bus stop. But he's a good guy."

I thank him and start walking.

"Be firm!" the policeman calls after me. "Keep reminding him to take you to the bus."

Belize City is a melting pot of old Maya history interwoven with Latino and indigenous Indian populations, people of Creole and Jamaican heritage, descendants of former African slaves, and the British who've been here since the early part of the seventeenth century. Some of the buildings are reminiscent of the British colonial period and have white clapboard walls and red roofs, while other structures are wooden shotgun houses on pilings that are painted tropical colors like peach and green or lemon yellow trimmed in blue.

Li Ho pharmacy is easy to find, and once inside I ask the

Asian man behind the counter if he knows of Taj. The man nods and points to a tall, beanstalk-looking guy with caramel-colored skin, who's wearing blue shorts and a T-shirt. Taj smiles big and nods. Two of his upper front teeth are gold, and most of his back ones are missing. The policeman was right: Taj looks like he's high on something.

His pupils have what I suspect is a permanent glazed look about them, and the whites of his eyes are yellowed as are three of the fingernails on his right hand. A sure sign he uses them to hold marijuana cigarettes when they're too short to hold any other way. I marvel at his hair, a wild unkempt forest of dread-locks that sprout in every diameter and length, along with parts of his beard that look like he bleached it but stopped short of adding color. Maybe it's because he's stoned, but Taj looks like a happy, don't worry kind of fellow.

"The policeman at the airport said you could take me to find the bus to Tikal."

Taj's smile covers his whole face. "He is my second cousin on my mother's side." His Jamaican accent is lilting and lyrical. "Yes. I will take you."

Before we leave, I buy a lined Big Chief tablet with a red cover, two pencils, fresh-cut mango in a clear plastic bag, three johnnycakes—think cornmeal flatbread—and a bottled orange drink. Before I can say anything, the Asian man behind the counter opens the orange drink, drops in a straw, and hands it to me.

Outside Taj points to his taxi, a small white car that looks like it hasn't been washed since the day it rolled off the assembly line. With dirt streets and water-filled potholes, I imagine there's not a lot of incentive for him to keep it clean.

It's midmorning and no one appears to be in a hurry. Clus-ters of indifferent chickens and roosters are poised on one foot, pecking at loose sand and gravel in the middle of the street. Next to them pedestrians have stopped and are talking to friends who're standing on pretty pink porches or leaning out of second-story windows. While the chickens and roosters have an inherent instinct for when to get out of the way, the people seem rooted in place. I imagine there may be a lot of pedestrian deaths in Belize City.

CHAPTER THIRTY-ONE

AS THE POLICEMAN PREDICTED, TAJ IS TRYING TO SELL me on the many benefits of his taxi, which include some smoke and a couple of his friends we could pick up along the way.

He eyes me in the rearview mirror and smiles. "They will show you a good time."

"No. Just the bus, please."

After several "important stops," I begin to wonder if the bus is actually running today. We've stopped at Steady Electronics to pick up a broken TV and Yellow Bird Discount Liquor to buy a pint of White Charcoal. The rum that "Picks You Up, Lifts You Up, and Keeps You Up," or so the sign in the store window says. I pass on a toke from Taj's cartoonish Cheech and Chong joint and the unidentified little orange balls he chews and then spits out of the car window and suggest a nice tip would be in order if he finds my bus in the next few minutes.

"Whatever you say, my lovely." He stops the taxi in the middle of the street long enough to put on a green, knitted Rasta cap and greet a fellow Jamaican.

In a few minutes Taj pulls up to another open market that runs alongside a different garbage-strewn canal. Mothers with big mesh bags are standing in line to buy onions, zucchini, and pineapples while their children stomp and play in the same rusty-colored water.

I grab my camera case while Taj pulls my canvas bag from the backseat and then walks me to an old yellow school bus. Tied to the roof are dozens of wire crates with live chickens, sacks of fruit, plastic jugs of petrol, and a guitar. Taj says the ride to San Ignacio, where I'll change to another bus to Tikal, will take two hours and cost $1.75 US. Before I board the bus, I thank him and pay him for the bus ride and his taxi, plus the tip I promised.

Just like the streets of Belize City, the inside of the bus is filled with an interesting assortment of people and smells. In the first row, near the door, sits an Asian man with unkempt whiskers that protrude from a mole on his chin, and he's wearing an enormous jade ring on his pinky finger. Some of the passengers behind him have high cheekbones and prominent noses, and I recognize them as descendants of the Maya.

As I make my way toward the back of the bus, I pass two teenage Black boys; several Indigenous people with shiny, straight black hair and skin the texture of oiled shoe leather; three little Black girls with brightly colored yarn on each of their pigtails; an Amish gentleman wearing black overalls and a straw hat, and now me. We are, indeed, an interesting group.

The bus isn't air-conditioned, and I settle into an empty seat next to an open window. Outside I see Taj has found someone else he knows, and they're laughing and talking and gesturing with their hands. He looks up and waves at me as the bus pulls away. I've gotten onboard just in time. It was as though the bus was waiting for me.

The bus leaves Belize City, and the driver turns onto a narrow, paved road bordered on both sides by a three-canopy jungle. I know from exploring the jungles in the Yucatán that, once inside, there are dense thickets of ferns and foliage and more species of birds and insects than I can count. Since the tree canopy prevents much of the sunlight from reaching the jungle floor, it's not uncommon for a tree to reach a height of eight stories tall as it struggles to seek its share of the light, plus the humidity and frequent rains supersize everything in the jungle. Like the trees in the Yucatán, I'm intrigued by the aerial roots of the giant ficus trees, some of which are as big around as the body of a sumo wrestler. They make my ficus trees in my living room look uncared for and anorexic.

Above the seat in front of me is a magnificent, almost regal-looking creature with long, arched, red and iridescent green tail feathers. I'm not sure, but it may be a fighting cock. The bird proceeds to claim the canvas bag I've thrown onto the overhead rack, and when I look up, he's peering down at me as though he's reconfirming that my bag is his seat for the duration of the journey. He has somewhat of an arrogant presence about him, and I decide he must be special because he's the only bird allowed inside the bus. The rest are in crates on the roof. I think his owner is the man sitting in front of me, because each time I look up at the bird, the man nods and smiles at me like a proud parent.

Everything on the bus strikes me as highly entertaining, and I'm beginning to wonder if some of the secondhand smoke from Taj's joint has made me stoned. Mounted over the bus's front window is a short red velvet curtain with red tassels that swing back and forth from the bottom of ornate scalloped edges. Above the curtain, a NO SMOKING sign and a NOT RESPONSIBLE FOR LOST ITEMS sign have been painted in English on the walls of the bus, and between them hang two hand-painted wooden statues of the Virgin Mary. Directly in front of the driver, another Virgin Mary is suction cupped to the front windshield and appears to be doing battle with a pink fuzzy Tweety bird affixed in the same manner. With so many distractions, I'm amazed the driver can concentrate on the road.

It's not long before I make friends with some of the children on the bus. A few are shy, but most are curious about the Anglo *gringa*. Three little girls have come and offered me peanuts and meat tacos made with strong juicy onions in exchange for pieces of my johnnycakes, and one of the girls just wants to sit next to me and touch my hair.

An overhead speaker plays American songs from the sixties like Bobby Vinton's "Mr. Lonely" and the Shangri-Las's "Leader of the Pack." "Sittin' on the Dock of the Bay" has been recorded in Spanish and sounds like it's been run through a reverberator in a large stone cathedral. It's corny and sweet, and I'm enjoying the music and the kids. This week has been a relief to feel so carefree. I'd almost forgotten what this state of being was like.

Perhaps it's the tunes Mr. Rooster likes because he's still there, perched on my bag like a king on his throne. His owner has turned in his seat to watch the children who've crowded around me in the aisle, and each time little liquid droppings from Mr. Rooster fall on my cheeks or my hair, his owner lights up like the bird just played Chopin. I hope this anointing means I've been blessed or something equally as benevolent.

When I'm no longer a novelty, the kids return to their seats. The driver has turned off the music, and the lack of sunlight and mile after mile of the rhythmic sound of the tires has lulled some of the passengers to sleep.

From time to time the jungle gives way to valleys of fertile farm fields and small thatched dwellings. In the distance, there's an expanse of rugged mountains, but for the most part, the jungle is the only thing I see. In its unspoken way, the thick jungle foliage is a clear KEEP OUT sign to the uninvited and uninitiated.

If the jungles of Belize and Guatemala are anything like those of the Yucatán, insects and birds thrive in the dense foliage along with predators like jaguars, bobcats, and deadly snakes that are camouflaged so well you won't see them until it's too late.

The bus has started making quick stops on the side of the road to let people off. At each stop, a little fellow in a blue shirt jumps off the bus, leaps onto the roof, and throws down the passengers' belongings, all done with lightning speed. He then drops from the roof, lets out a yelp, and the bus begins pulling away. Each time, when I think he won't catch up to the bus, I see him running alongside, as fast as he can, and seconds before the bus leaves him behind, he grabs ahold of the doorway and swings his body inside. It seems to be a game between the man and the driver.

When the bus stops again, this time there's only me and two other passengers left on board, and the driver tells me I need to get off.

"I'm going to Tikal," I tell him.

"*Otro autobús, mañana,*" the driver says. Another bus will be along tomorrow to take me to Tikal.

Taj didn't say anything about waiting until tomorrow for the next bus. "I can't stay here until tomorrow," I tell the driver.

"*San Ignacio es asi,*" the driver says. He points behind us in the direction we've just come.

I don't remember passing a town or even seeing a sign. "Can you take me back to San Ignacio? I'll pay you."

"*No, señora.*"

I'm feeling uneasy about getting off and being left on the side of the road, but I can tell the driver and the fellow in the blue shirt are eager to leave. To motivate my departure, the driver puts the bus in gear and moves it forward a few feet. I take my camera case and my canvas bag and get off and watch them as the bus drives away.

CHAPTER THIRTY-TWO

ON BOTH SIDES OF THE ROAD, THE JUNGLE IS THICK and impenetrable looking, and like the other jungles I'm familiar with, this one grows to the edge of the road. The green labyrinth is alive with the sound of birds and monkeys, but other than the whistles and screeches from the wildlife, I hear nothing that indicates there's a nearby town.

Perhaps I should've asked Taj more questions about the bus schedules, but the place where I'd boarded wasn't a formal bus station. It was just a bus parked next to a bustling marketplace with no place to post schedules of arrivals and departures. Philip and I have been to Belize, and we've traveled to Mexico more times than I can remember, so I know it's just how they do things in this part of the world. I'd taken Taj's word the bus would stop in San Ignacio where I could catch another bus to Tikal. When I'd asked him how long I'd be in San Ignacio he'd replied, "Not long, my lovely." There'd been nothing to worry about. No red flags. If anything, I was excited to be on my own. To become the adventurous Ramborella again.

With my canvas bag in one hand and my camera case slung over the other shoulder, I start walking in the same direction as the two passengers who got off before me. Perhaps they're going to San Ignacio as well, but before I can catch up to them, they turn and disappear into the jungle. When I reach the place where they turned off the road, I see nothing but a narrow green trail that melds into the shadows and then disappears into the darkened undergrowth.

Usually I'm better prepared with information about where I'm going and how to get there, but the decision to visit Tikal had been last minute. In addition to Mexico and Belize, Philip and I took numerous trips to the Virgin Islands and different islands in the Bahamas but never without a plan. This time I have no traveling companions and no plan, and to say I'm uneasy about being out here alone is an understatement. I feel exposed and vulnerable but more than anything, I'm defenseless. It's me and the wall-to-wall jungle, and if a four-legged or a two-legged predator were to come after me, there's no safe place for me to hide.

Up ahead, there's a narrow clearing on the side of the road and a small, weather-worn sign that says "San Ignacio." I follow the clearing to a dirt street and a handful of cinder-block buildings that are set back from the main road. The structures are all closed and shuttered, as though the town has been abandoned.

It's not long before I see a small red-and-white four-door car with the word *Taxi* on the side. The driver is the only person inside. He stops and asks where I'm going.

"The bus from Belize City dropped me off a little while ago. I'm supposed to catch another bus in San Ignacio that will take me to Tikal."

The driver shakes his head. "*No señora. No más* bus today."

"No señora" seems to be the phrase of the day. I've heard it twice in less than twenty minutes.

"For $10 US, I take you to *la frontera*. You catch bus."

"*Que es la frontera?*" I ask.

"La frontera . . . Belize *y* Guatemala. *Es trece kilómeters, más o menos."*

The driver is telling me it's thirteen kilometers to the border between Belize and Guatemala where I'll be able to catch another bus. The man is small in stature and looks like he could be in his fifties. He has a kind face, but then Ted Bundy had a benign face as well. If any of his victims could have had a do-over, I'm sure all of them would have run the other way as fast as they could. I consider my options, but other than walking farther down a nothing dirt road, it appears as though I have none.

I've done a lot of dangerous things, but I've never accepted a ride from a stranger . . . in the middle of nowhere . . . in another country. Taj was recommended by the policeman at the airport, and we'd been surrounded by people in Belize City. I hope this taxi driver is on the up and up as well because other than sitting on my bag all night in a place that's not much more than a pit stop in the jungle, I'm not sure what else to do.

"Bueno," I tell him. *"Muchas gracias."* I toss my bags into the back seat and slide in beside them.

The driver is a talkative sort who tells me his name is Carlos, a retired mahogany craftsman who drives a taxi in Guatemala City and comes home to San Ignacio when he can. He has a young wife and small children. I'm surprised his English is as good as it is, although if he drives a taxi in Guatemala City, I imagine he meets a lot of English-speaking people.

I take a deep breath and decide to relax. At least I'm not in a house with a cocaine lab and a husband who's lost control.

The term *frontier* makes me think about the American Wild West and the early settlers who ventured forth on horseback and covered wagons to make new lives for themselves and settle a land they'd never seen. I, too, need to make a new life, but compared to them I have it easy. I'm riding in a taxi.

In a couple of miles the paved road has turned into an obstacle course filled with large rocks and rubble. Carlos stops the car and talks to me over his shoulder. "We no go here. I show you." He sits upright, as tall as he can, and moves closer to the steering wheel. The rocks under the tires are now big boulders and our drive has become slow and tedious. Carlos is peering over the hood of his car, trying to navigate around the substantial obstructions in our path.

The road we're on isn't much wider than a single lane, and we're climbing in elevation. On one side of us is a mountain that goes straight up. On the other side I can see land and the countryside several hundred feet below.

Carlos stops the car and turns off the engine and motions for me to get out of the car. "I show you."

Alarm bells are going off in my head. Big red alarms with blaring sirens! *What if he's going to rob me and push me over the edge of the road?* I begin to evaluate my next move. If he tries something, then he's going to have to do it with me in the back seat, because I'm not getting out of the taxi.

Carlos opens the back passenger door on the side of the car that plunges straight down the mountain. He looks to be at least five, maybe six inches shorter than me. I lean back and ready myself to push him over the edge of the mountain with a swift kick of my legs. He sees my reaction and leaves the door open and walks toward the front of the car.

"*Aqui.*" He points to the ground with both hands. "*El terremoto.*" He grimaces and shakes his hands and upper body and then points at something in front of the car. "We no go here."

I ease myself out of the back seat and take three or four steps forward to where Carlos is nodding and pointing. There's a deep crevasse that's maybe five feet across and runs the width of the road. Unless he's Evel Knievel, the chasm's too wide for him to drive across to the other side. He picks up a rock and drops it into the abyss. I watch, waiting to hear it land, but there is nothing but silence.

"*El terremoto*. Is that an earthquake?"

Carlos nods affirmatively, happy I've understood him.

"So, we can't go this way."

Still smiling, he nods once more in confirmation. "*Comprendo*. We go other road."

I nod, relieved he hasn't brought me here to rob me or kill me, but I don't understand why he's done this. Why would he bring me miles out of our way to show me the regular route is impassible?

He motions for me to stand against the mountainside as he backs up and then drives forward, turning his tires a little more each time until he's turned the car around. Then he signals for me to get back inside, and he retraces the way we came, following the mountain down to the main road where he turns left.

This part of the road is rocky and strewn with boulders bigger than any of the ones we've encountered so far, and Carlos is unable to do anything but creep along and pick his way around them as though they are hidden bombs in danger of going off. Like many of the roads in Mexico and Central America, the road here is narrow, not wide enough for two lanes. At this glacial pace, it could take all afternoon to get to the Guatemalan border.

We've been on the rubble-strewn road for at least forty-five minutes when I see the first signs of civilization since San Ignacio. Carlos stops the car so I can get a better look. In front of us is a big billboard like the ones on the side of the highways in the United States, except this one is only a few feet off the ground. Plastered across the front is a foreboding image of a skull and crossbones—the universal sign for poison—and perched on top of the skull is a maroon and black military beret. Instead of the traditional crossbones, two automatic weapons have taken their place, and underneath the skull in big, black letters are the words "*INFIERNO. NO ENTRAR.*" HELL. DO NOT ENTER.

Carlos turns his head to look at me. "*Aquí.*" He's pointing to a road that intersects the one we're on. "Other road." He nods like he wants me to agree with him, and then turns right at the entrance to Hell, but I haven't agreed to anything. I've already been to Hell, and I don't want to go back.

Like the other roads I've been on today, this one cuts a narrow swath through the jungle, but this road is gravel, and there are no giant boulders to slow us down. The taxi's tires leave a wake of brown dust behind us, and I can hear the small rocks as they crunch beneath the rubber.

To my left is a tall wooden lookout tower with a man inside. As he peers down at us, I can see he's holding an automatic weapon. His face is expressionless. A short distance beyond the guard tower, I see part of what looks like an obstacle course with monkey bars and footbridges made of ropes and another foreboding sign. This one is yellow with black icons of helicopters followed by exclamation marks and something in Spanish I don't understand, but it's the next thing I see that makes it difficult to breathe. Outside my window, shallow graves are lined end-to-end, each with a fresh mound of dirt on top—a crude cemetery inside the gates of Hell.

Up ahead on the right, several men have emerged from the jungle, and one of them is motioning for us to stop. They are soldiers dressed in khaki camouflage uniforms and black leather boots. Their short shirt sleeves are rolled up like 1950s American greasers and just like the skull on the billboard, they're wearing maroon and black berets and carrying machine guns. Their faces are hard, and their eyes are as impregnable as a bulletproof vest. They are the soldiers from *Infierno*. The soldiers from Hell.

Another soldier appears out of the jungle and approaches the passenger side of the taxi. He looks at me in the back seat, then at the driver, and back at me again. He eyes the inside of the car, checking the floorboards in the front and back seats, then reaches inside the open window to the glove compartment and rifles through a handful of papers. At the same time, another soldier beats twice on the trunk with his fist. Carlos inhales and holds his breath for a moment. His exhale is shaky and irregular, but he gets out and opens the trunk.

Inside my little voice is screaming *we need to get out of here*, but on the outside I'm calm and collected. I remember how my little voice screamed at me before Philip knocked me to the floor and choked me, but I didn't have the foresight to run. Now I have no place to run. No window to jump out of, and I'm surrounded by soldiers carrying automatic weapons.

The lead soldier closes the glove compartment and steps toward the rear passenger door. He nods at me and puts both hands together like he's opening an imaginary book. I'm guessing he wants to see my passport, but before I can retrieve it, he shifts his weight and reaches his arm past me through the open window. His breath smells like cigarettes and onions, and he lifts the top of my camera case and removes my passport. He studies my photo, and then me, and with my passport in hand, he turns and walks back into the jungle.

I've traveled the Mexican outback enough to know that sometimes you get stopped by bandits who rob you and then let you go. I remember the money inside my camera case the soldier didn't find. Almost a hundred Belize dollars. If need be, perhaps they'll take it and allow us to be on our way.

Two of the remaining armed men approach the taxi. One of them rests his arms on the open window next to me and begins running the back of his fingers down my bare arm. His hand pauses to rest on my shoulder, and he cocks his head and arches one eyebrow.

He's handsome, in a rugged sort of way, but more than anything he's confident, and I can tell he thinks he's a ladies' man. A Romeo. The soldier two steps behind him is thin and wiry, and something about his eyes tells me he's hopped up on something. Coffee or cocaine. Maybe both. Another soldier with a machine gun stands ten feet away from him, and he hasn't moved since they emerged from the jungle.

With his eyes still on mine, Romeo steps back from the car. I notice a two-inch scar on the right side of his face, starting at the top of his cheekbone. He inhales and tilts his head back ever so slightly, and with the faintest hint of a smile, he turns and, together with the Wiry One, disappears into the jungle. The soldier with the machine gun, the one with dead eyes who looks like a hard ass, stays where he is. Watching us.

CHAPTER THIRTY-THREE

THE HEAT INSIDE THE TAXI IS STIFLING AND TRICKLES OF sweat are running down the nape of my neck to the small of my back, but I take comfort that Carlos hasn't turned off the engine. In a little while I'll get my passport back and we'll be on our way.

Carlos is staring straight ahead and has begun talking softly like he's muttering to himself. I lean forward so I can hear him better.

"*Que?*" I ask. "*No comprendo.*" My Spanish is basic. Good for asking directions, ordering food, and telling a mother her little girl is pretty.

"*Mi esposa* . . . she no forgives me."

Carlos continues to stare straight ahead and once again I'm surprised by how well he speaks English.

"She feed you. You sleep. I take you for bus *mañana*." He looks at me in the rearview mirror. His eyes are afraid. "*Lo siento* . . . I sorry." His apology hangs in the air like a condolence at a funeral.

Nothing about this place feels right or safe, and Hard-Ass over there hasn't moved in a long time. He's still standing with his legs spread wide, holding his automatic weapon at a forty-five-degree angle to his body. If he's trying to look scary, he's doing a stellar job.

I don't know if he can hear or understand us, but like Carlos, I keep my voice low. *"Dónde estamos?"* I ask him. "Where are we?"

"Los militares. Guatemala commandos." He whispers the words like he's spoken the name of the devil. He nods his head in the direction of the shallow graves. *"Niños. Doce. Trece. Los Desaparecidos."* It sounds as though he's on the verge of tears, and he shakes his head with an almost imperceptible nod. "Never know."

"Guatemala?" I ask. *"No comprendo."* I thought he was driving me to the frontier, the border between Belize and Guatemala where I could catch a bus, but I believe he's saying we're already in Guatemala.

"Sus padres . . . never know . . . *Sus madres . . .* never know. Disappear."

The words *commando* and *disappear* rocket shockwaves through my body. This must be what it feels like to be struck by lightning. If I understand him correctly, the shallow graves next to us on the road are those of young boys, twelve and thirteen years old, taken by the Guatemalan commandos. The same men who've stopped us and taken my passport. If they do this to children, what will they do to me?

"Trabajar en los campos de adormideras," Carlos continues.

"I don't understand," I whisper. "The boys worked where?"

Carlos nods his head in the direction of the road up ahead. *"Amapola.* Poppies."

I came to Belize to reset everything back to zero, before the Valium incident and the drug lab in the dungeon. To have fun and reconnect with the adventurous parts of myself I've lost, but now I want to cry out for help. I want Philip. Healthy Philip. The one who, if the world were coming to an end, would figure a way around it. But he isn't here, and I'm in the middle of nowhere. In

Hell. With soldiers who kidnap and kill young boys. Children who will never go home, whose parents will never know what happened to them, and now I learn there are poppies in Hell as well. Opium. Morphine. Heroin. The devil's calling cards.

Everything's falling into place. Why Carlos was so insistent on showing me why the regular route was impassible. His fear, and now mine, is as unmistakable as thunder.

My heart has started fluttering. It's my mitral valve prolapse. The floppy valve in my heart that either lets in too much blood or not enough. Sometimes it's stress-related, and it makes me dizzy and light-headed like I'm going to faint. I can't deal with this now.

Other than sitting here, waiting, I consider the alternatives. We could put the car in gear and floor it, but Carlos doesn't strike me as having the nerve to do that. Besides, there's Hard-Ass a few feet away and the armed commando in the top of the guard tower behind us. Any stray vestiges of hope that we'll leave here safely are beginning to evaporate like raindrops in Hell.

What a dumb shit! I'm such a dumb shit! This morning I stepped through a wormhole without thinking about anything except wanting to see Tikal. When I was twenty-one, Tulum had been my first ruin, and like the devil's other drugs, for me, one ruin is never enough.

Since the first time I saw Tulum, I've studied the architecture of the Maya, their calendar, the gods they worshipped, and the jade beads they put in the mouths of their dead, but the dead boys in the shallow graves beside me don't have jade beads in their mouths. Only bullets. Or maybe their heads were bashed in by the butt of a gun or a shovel while they worked in the poppy fields.

Whether they're made from poppies, or they're cocaine, alcohol, and nicotine, I understand dangerous drugs, and I've known for some time my drug is the adrenaline that comes from putting myself in challenging situations like racing cars and landing on aircraft carriers. Like the Sirens, the beautiful but dangerous creatures of Greek mythology who lured sailors to their doom, my Sirens have beckoned me onward and dared me to become the opposite of the sickly little girl who couldn't play outside. Being an adrenaline junkie makes you think you can do anything and go anywhere. What if I've come to believe that, but this time, my sirens have led me to my doom?

Hard-Ass is still standing in the same spot, and Carlos is rambling, repeating things he's already said. "I drive in Guatemala City. Money for *mi esposa y niñas.*"

He's calmer when he's talking about his family, and I need him to remain calm, so I ask him to tell me about his children. Some are in their twenties and thirties and two are under ten.

"*Muy difícil. Mi esposa* es young woman. I work for them."

I don't know how much time has elapsed, but the commandos aren't back with my passport. I don't know if this is a good sign or a bad one, but my thoughts keep getting stuck on worst case, and rape is the only thing that comes to mind. If things get out of hand, I need Carlos to see me as more than a fare in the back seat of his taxi. I need him to care about what happens to me.

"*Mi nombre es* Brenda," I tell him.

For the first time since we've been sitting here, he turns around in his seat and looks at me. He manages a weak smile. "*Mees Brain-da. Me llamo* Estéban."

"But you said your name was Carlos."

He looks down with a sheepish expression. "Carlos easy for tourists. I am Estéban."

Three commandos we haven't seen before have come out of the jungle. All of them are carrying machine guns. One of them opens the back door and motions for me to get out, while another one goes around and opens Estéban's door. Someone turns off the taxi's engine, and I hear the jangling of car keys. I hope Estéban has pocketed them, but I fear he doesn't have that kind of courage.

With the end of his machine gun, one of the commandos motions for me to walk toward Hard-Ass, who's waiting to lead us into the jungle. There's something so final about it all like we won't be coming back here. *Oh, God, help me!* No one knows where I am, and the only proof I was here is my canvas bag and the camera case with my name on it in the backseat of Estéban's taxi.

I stand motionless. *Don't follow them.* Every instinct tells me to run the other way. *You can't go with them!* I turn to look at Estéban in time to see him physically getting smaller. His head drops, his shoulders slump, and the vertebrae in his back look as though they've collapsed one onto the other. A defeated man going to his execution.

Hard-Ass is the first one to step inside the jungle. Another commando follows him while the one behind me pushes hard against my back with the barrel of his automatic weapon. He's signaling me to start walking. High overhead a group of toucans croak and scream, warning one another. Or maybe they're warning me.

CHAPTER THIRTY-FOUR

THE TRAIL WE'RE ON LOOKS LIKE A GREEN TUNNEL hollowed out through the middle of the jungle. I know from exploring the jungles in the Yucatán that without foot traffic, it won't be long before parts of the jungle grow back as though the trail never existed. In places, the canopy arches just above our heads while in other areas the trees are like skyscrapers, too tall for me to see the tops. Sometimes I can see pieces of the sky, but it's the opposite of Tulum and *Sian Ka'an*, the Maya words for "the place where the sky was born." This is not where the sky was born.

The commandos are all wearing boots while I have on my white Keds, still wet from the saltwater on Ambergris Caye. Under my feet I'm aware of the layers and layers of rotting plants, the place in the jungle where dead things go. From experience I know there are snakes in the jungle. Some are harmless while others, like the deadly fer-de-lance, are well-camouflaged, impossible to see until you're almost on top of them.

The commando behind me has his hand on my back and each time I hesitate to take a step, he shoves me forward. Walking here isn't easy. The tree roots in our path are sometimes two feet high, and I'm forced to watch every step. I know from exploring the jungle: if you get lost, there's a chance you may never find your way out.

Hard-Ass and the commando in front of me haven't stopped since we started walking. I turn to see if Estéban is still behind me. He's breathing hard, and his face and shirt are wet. With a quick movement, the commando behind me jerks his head up and back—a sign for me to turn around and keep walking. Like Estéban, my shirt is wet and sticking to my skin, and small tendrils of wet hair have plastered themselves to the side of my face.

Overhead, the jungle's alarm system continues to announce our presence. The loudest warning is the cacophony of howler monkeys, and the sound they make is frightening and unnerving. A combination of wild barking dogs and angry hooting gorillas. Up ahead a large bird screeches, together with lots of high-pitched tweets from smaller birds, and there are rhythmic sounds I can't identify. They remind me of the rain sticks the Native Americans use to summon rain from the heavens, but rain isn't the problem here. It's the other commandos who are waiting for us somewhere up ahead.

Black ants have crawled up my shoes and are biting my ankles. I stop to reach down and flick them off, and I'm met with a swarm of mosquitos and tiny flying things that rise from the rotting layers beneath my feet. The mosquitos and flying things cover my arms and face and bore into my nostrils and ears. Like a crazy person, I begin swatting and smacking my face and then, just as suddenly, they vanish without a trace.

In a small clearing a few feet away, I notice a line of the same black ants. There are thousands of them. A militia of ants moving collectively, jostling one on top of and around one another as one, a long movable chain that appears to stay in the same place. They're making a humming sound together with something that sounds like a clicking noise.

The jungle is the perfect place to do unspeakable things. If the commandos don't get me, the insects will, or maybe they'll take over after the commandos are finished with me. Maybe I'll become a part of the rotting ecosystem on the jungle floor.

Hard-Ass stops and raises a hand like he's heard something. Ahead of us in a larger clearing, I see fallen trees as long and as big around as telephone poles, lying at odd angles to one another. Overhead I'm aware the spider monkeys have stopped as well. They've been following us, leaping from tree to tree, hanging by the same freakishly long tails and arms as the monkeys I saw my first time in the jungle near Tulum. Their cries are an unnerving combination of deep-throated whippoorwills and women screaming.

Grateful for the rest, I listen for whatever Hard-Ass thinks he hears. I hear nothing but the sounds of the jungle. I try to memorize the clearing and the way the big trees have fallen. I don't know what I'll do with this knowledge but as with Philip and the men who broke into our house, I'm the only one I can count on.

My clothes are wet, and a large piece of hair has dropped in front of my eyes. The ends are dripping with sweat and humidity, and I can't remember the last time I had something to drink. Perhaps it was the bottled orange drink I bought at Li Ho pharmacy a lifetime ago.

Except for short comments to one another in Spanish, the commandos say nothing. I'm more convinced than ever, if their intentions were good, they would've told us where we were going and why. On the other hand, maybe they want me to answer questions about where I'm going and how long I'll be there—but they could have done that back at Estéban's taxi.

I tell myself, *Whatever happens . . . I'll be okay.* I've dealt with a lot in my life, and I'm made of tougher stuff than almost anyone I know. I think of my friend who, as part of his Army Ranger training, was dropped in the freezing snowy woods with no clothes, no shoes, and no supplies—a winter ranger—and had to make his way back to civilization. Perhaps I'll become a "summer ranger."

Most of the people who know me don't know how tough I am. They don't have a clue what life with Philip was like, and those who know just *think* they know. They don't know what it's like to go without sleep for fear of a chemical reaction going wrong or the house catching on fire. What it's like to live with, and witness, a loved one's daily transformation into a stranger, but freaking out has never been my nature.

I don't scream. I don't cry. I'm the opposite of the women I see in B-grade horror films. The ones who panic and scream and stay rooted in place with their hands on either side of their face, like they're stuck there with super glue, as the monster lumbers toward them. I carry on until the crisis is behind me, and even then, I don't complain and rarely give way to my emotions.

I manage to catch Estéban's gaze. Emotionally and physically, he's shut down. Void of all hope and fight should I need him. My heart is skipping beats again. Two fast ones, then I miss one, followed by two or three normal beats, but I give Estéban a faint smile. My shoulders are back, and my head is high. "Gather your strength," I want to tell him, but I'm not sure how much he has left. Life here is hard, and I don't know how much he's already gathered to provide for his family. A lot, I suspect.

Estéban didn't say what happened to his first wife, but divorce isn't common in this part of the world, and I don't believe he's the kind of man to have a *chica de casa*—a wife at home—and a girlfriend on the side. Since his wife is younger, I'm wondering if the mother of his older children died.

Estéban is a good man. I know he is, but I'm having a hard

time reconciling why he brought me this way. He must've known the commandos would stop us. Was this the only other route? What if we hadn't turned right at the entrance to Hell and stayed straight on the road we'd been on? And the buses that go to the frontier . . . Do they come this way as well? Or maybe the commandos let big buses full of people pass through, but not American gringas, traveling alone.

Hard-Ass is moving forward again. In a little while I see a clearing up ahead in front of what appears to be part of an un-restored Maya temple. Over time, giant tree roots have forced their way between the temple stones and broken them apart, and the pieces are strewn haphazardly along the ground. The temple is covered in vines and trees, making it impossible to tell how big it is. This ruin has been here for thousands of years, but in the end, I know the jungle always wins. I hope this isn't a portent of the things that will happen to me.

I turn to look at Estéban. He's stepped into the clearing behind me, and he looks like the cowardly lion who's been brought to stand before the great Oz. If need be, I doubt whether he'll find his voice to ask for courage.

In the middle of the vines and massive tree roots, I see a small opening in the side of the temple. It's big enough for someone Estéban's size to almost stand up and large enough for several people to sit inside and stay dry during the frequent jungle rains. I wonder if it's the beginning of an internal passageway that leads to a Maya king's burial tomb. When I look closer, I notice it's littered with beer and soda bottles. Hardly befitting the surroundings of a king.

With the end of his machine gun, Hard-Ass points to a large round stone and gestures to me and Estéban. "*Siéntate,*" he barks. I think it means "sit," but whatever he said, it was a command, not a request.

Estéban's legs are rubbery, and he looks terrified like he's expecting the worst will happen any second now. He collapses onto the stone, and I sit down beside him. I need to stay in control, but like Estéban, my fears are beginning to get the best of me. It feels like we're their captives, and I can't think of anything but what they're going to do with us, or is it just to me.

My heart continues to beat out of rhythm, and I remind myself to stay calm and breathe. *Just breathe.* I hear the sound of car keys, and I notice one of the commandos has handed Hard-Ass what I believe are the keys to the taxi.

Off to one side of the crumbling ruin is a tall, limestone stela stone. Like a history book, stela stones document Maya rulers, how they conquered their enemies, and the ceremonies they performed like bloodletting rituals and human sacrifices, offered as powerful nourishment to the gods. Some of the hieroglyphics and carved relief figures on this stone are still visible, particularly the ones painted Maya blue, a vibrant and indestructible pigment, a color that's lasted for centuries. I'm reminded that it's also the shade they painted the bodies of their living sacrificial offerings and that most of them were women.

A few yards away, the carvings on another stela stone are more intact. I can make out the clear profile of a face, an eye, and a prominent Maya nose, and on top of the figure's head is what looks like a serpent with its tongue out. The meaning of these stones and the possible reasons we were brought here have not escaped me: What if I become a sacrifice to their carnal cravings? For most of my adult life, I've offered myself to a man I loved and worshiped like a god, and now, savage murderous commandos have taken me against my will. I can only hope I'm as indestructible and resilient as the color Maya blue.

At any other time and place, I would've been ecstatic to find two stela stones and a partially excavated temple, but there's no awe or excitement coursing through my veins. I'm not filled with wonder, only vivid reminders of the Maya's brutal heritage, a hierarchy of behavior like the Guatemalan military commandos and their victims in the shallow graves. The boys who are now *los desaparecidos*.

When they weren't farming poppies or making cuts in the seed pods and scraping the milky fluid to be dried and sold as opium gum, I wonder if the boys had hacked away this part of the temple's jungle facade. Boys who, if they didn't perform well, were killed. I can't unsee their crude end-to-end resting places. They will stay with me as long as I live. However long that may be.

CHAPTER THIRTY-FIVE

THE COMMANDOS WHO FORCED US INTO THE JUNGLE are standing side by side, smoking cigarettes. If they say anything to one another it's only a word or two here and there I don't understand, but by their demeanor, I get the impression we're waiting for someone. The person who will decide what to do with us.

When I was sitting in the taxi, it was hard to think about anything other than the shallow graves on the road beside me. Now all I can focus on is why they've brought us here, and the one answer I keep coming back to is that I'm to become their *puta*. Their whore. Maybe I'm for the man we're waiting for, or maybe they'll keep me as their sex slave with each man taking his turn again and again until there's nothing left of me that interests them. Or like the hieroglyphics on the tombs of the Maya kings, perhaps they'll sacrifice me to an unknown god because they can. Because in some twisted way, they get off on it.

I want one of them to look me in the eyes. I need to know what they're thinking, and whether I can spot any clues about what's going to happen to us. I wouldn't be the first woman to be gang-raped until there was nothing left of her, but if I'm right, is this something I want to know in advance?

While this was happening to other women, I wonder if they

fought back, or did they have no choice but to lie there with their eyes closed? And what did they do with their thoughts? Did they disconnect and go someplace else in their mind? Is that a survival mechanism that kicks in by itself, or will I have to beg God to make my mind go blank?

It seems like an hour has passed since Estéban and I've been sitting here on the large stone block when somewhere through the trees ahead I hear voices. The commandos take one last draw from their cigarettes and then stub them out on the ground with the toe of their boots.

The one we've been waiting for has arrived and Romeo is with him. The man is older than the others, and the only one not wearing a beret, but it's clear he's the one in charge. He is El Jefe. His face is wide, punctuated by two heavy black eyebrows and a thick black mustache, and he has a pistol strapped low around his waist.

I can feel my heart beating in my fingertips and my mouth has gone dry, but I can't let them know how terrified I am. I don't want them to think I will go willingly into whatever they have planned for me. I sit up tall and look him in the eyes.

El Jefe studies me as Hard-Ass steps forward and hands him my passport. El Jefe flips through it thoughtfully, looking at each of the many stamps inside: Tampico. Cancún. Oaxaca. Monterrey. Miami. Nassau. London. Geneva. Paris. Tuxtla Gutiérrez. Mexico City. Belize. Maybe I should tell him I'm not traveling alone. My husband and our friends are behind us, and they'll see our taxi on the side of the road; but it sounds weak, like something I made up, so I stay silent.

It's clear El Jefe isn't interested in Estéban. He doesn't ask his name or why we were on the dusty brown road next to the shallow graves. People like Estéban are disposable commodities like chewing gum and toilet tissue.

El Jefe's demeanor is that of someone who has many things that require his time. He's all business, and I get the impression I'm an inconvenient interruption. Not high enough on his priority list to require his personal attention. That's a good thing, I hope. Maybe he'll let us go.

He turns his back to me and starts talking to Romeo and Hard-Ass. I look on as Romeo nods his head in agreement and at the same time, snatches quick glimpses of me out of the corner of his eyes. My ears are ringing, and I'm filled with this sick feeling of dread. What if El Jefe has decided I'm a form of entertainment for his men? Like when Bob Hope brought girls to remote outposts in Korea and Vietnam to bolster troop morale, except I won't be singing and dancing.

The small wiry commando, the one who looks like he's high on something, moves closer to hear what the others are saying. He looks eager, too eager, like he's waiting for something big to happen at any moment.

El Jefe hands my passport to Hard-Ass, who then gives it to the Wiry One, who drops it on a stone block carved into the shape of a serpent's head. The stone is in the shadows, but one thing jumps out at me. My passport. The familiar blue book with the gold seal of the United States of America has landed next to Estéban's keys.

Somewhere in the distance, the staccato sound of machine-gun fire drowns out the chorus of birds and howler monkeys. First a short burst, then another, followed by a single pistol shot, and then silence. As he takes off running in the direction of the shots, El Jefe motions for Hard-Ass and the rest of the men who brought us here to follow him.

Romeo and the Wiry One stay behind, and within seconds, Romeo orders him to follow the others. "*Siguelos!*" he shouts. The Wiry One, happy to have a place to channel his energy, runs after them, and like the others, he disappears into the jungle.

Romeo is the only commando left with me and Estéban, and the look on his face telegraphs more than I want to know. He walks toward me, his eyes fixed on mine, and with one swift move, he pulls me up by my hands until we are face-to-face.

His eyes are excited. Greedy looking. They scan my face, down my neck, and across my breasts like they don't know which part of me to focus on first, but I know. He's going to rape me. Here. Now. He's going to do unspeakable things to me.

He runs his fingers down the side of my neck. Then he cocks his head the way he did back at the car. He's been waiting for this moment since he first saw me. Without warning, Romeo grunts and shoves me to the ground. He drops down, his knees pinned against either side of me, and pushes up my T-shirt and my bra and exposes my breasts. His hands are all over me, running down my midriff and my navel to the top of my jeans.

"Get off!" I squirm back and forth like a bucking horse, trying to throw its rider. I hit his arms and face with my closed fists as I try to wrestle my body out from under him, but he's unfazed. He's too strong for me. He's pinned me to the ground, and I'm trapped between his powerful legs. I claw at his face, down the scar I first noticed when he walked out of the jungle.

He unzips my jeans and yanks them and my underwear down over my hips as his fingernails tear gashes in my flesh. Romeo unbuckles the pistol holster around his waist and tosses it on the ground beside him and unzips his camouflage pants. With both hands, he shoves them down to his knees and exposes himself. His penis is hard, and I can tell the only thing he's thinking about is putting it inside of me. He spreads my legs and stares at my vagina like he's found a cache of Maya gold.

He's lost in the moment, looking down at himself and the

view of his penis as it towers over me. He's proud of it and takes pleasure in looking at its erect state. He thrusts his pelvis back and forth in midair, simulating what he's going to do to me. Everything has fallen off his radar except what it's going to feel like when he gets inside me and starts pumping away. How good it will feel when he cums in me.

I twist and thrash, fighting to push him away when my hand brushes against his penis. He shudders with pleasure and his head goes back. Eyes closed. He likes that I have touched him, and he keeps thrusting at the air, hoping I'll touch him again. I'm not getting out of here alive, but I don't have to go willingly. I would rather die, now, attempting to get away, than after he and the other commandos have had their turn with me.

Romeo's penis is hard and curves upward, and his testicles hang down, firm and taut—ready to explode. I seize the moment and reach underneath his penis and grab them. I squeeze as hard as I can, twisting them with all my might, digging my fingernails into his flesh, and trying to rip them from his body. All my anger over Philip and the corporate thieves at the savings and loan has found a worthy target, and I'm focused on hurting Romeo as much as I can.

Romeo lets out a scream. It shifts into a low guttural growl that sounds like a wounded animal, and he falls on his side, doubled up in pain. He looks at me with a wide-eyed, incredulous look like he's seeing me for the first time. Not my body parts and how good they can make him feel, but me. His face is washed in pain and surprise and flashes of anger. Both hands cover his groin, and he's groaning and rocking back and forth in the fetal position.

I jump up and pull on my jeans. He raises his head and looks up at me, and I kick him as hard as I can in the middle of his throat. His hands fly to his neck, and he's gasping, trying to inhale, but I've taken his breath away. He rolls onto his back. His legs are splayed and his groin is exposed, and with everything I have, I kick him hard. Once, twice, in rapid succession, like I'm busting down a door with my foot.

His pistol holster is on the ground behind him. I take a wide step around his body and lean down and grab his gun from the holder. It's my protection should he or the others come after me. I'm not sure how far away they are, but the gunshots I heard earlier sounded like it would take a minute or more for anyone to get there.

The keys and my passport are on the serpent stone. I scoop them up and stick the passport in the waistband of my jeans and the keys in my front pocket. Romeo's pistol is in my right hand.

I think Estéban's been on his feet for most of this, but I'm not sure.

"*Vámonos!*" I tell him. "Run!"

Estéban stands motionless. I don't know whether he's scared or in shock, but I grab his hand and pull him along, running down the same path that brought us here. This time I'm running with no regard for pit vipers in the leaves or big black ants because if we don't make it to the car before Romeo sounds the alarm or comes after us, we're dead.

I'm running faster than Estéban, and I lose hold of his hand. I pause long enough to grab it again. We pass the clearing with the undulating trail of moving ants. When we were being led into the jungle, I tried to pay attention. Were there any other paths or was this the main one? There had been only one other worn footpath, and it was perpendicular to this one, near the fallen trees. I'm certain we're going in the right direction. We're on the path that will lead us to the road and Estéban's taxi.

Both of us stumble and fall at the same time. We've tripped over the roots of a giant tree. The roots are tall and thin, and their shape reminds me of oversized oars on a fishing boat. I've scraped the palm of my hand, and one of my wrists is gouged and bleeding, but at least I didn't fall on the pistol and shoot one of us. Estéban's lower lip has busted open, and blood is pouring down his chin.

The mosquitos and the flying things along the rotting jungle floor are buzzing around my face and neck. I get up and pull Estéban to his feet. He hasn't said a word since we got out of the taxi. I believe he's in shock, but I can't let go of his hand because he'll stay rooted in place until the devils from Hell come for him.

"*Vámonos*," I say, again.

I hear something behind us that sounds like a person or a large animal running through the brush. What if it's Romeo and the other commandos? I know I hurt him, badly, but I also know his sexist machismo won't let him give in to his pain because I've shamed him. He can't let me, a mere woman, his captive and his whore, get away with hurting his penis and his pride, but more than that, I suspect he fears El Jefe's reaction when he learns we've gotten away. I will have humiliated them all.

High overhead, the howler monkeys are making a deafening chorus of calls. Like lions roaring, screaming as though *they* are the ones who've been assaulted, they're sounding a warning to the others. *Danger!* Maybe they're reacting to me and Estéban, running through the trees beneath them, but I can't be sure.

Back there somewhere I know Romeo is on his feet, and he's coming after us, but I have his pistol. When he approached me at the car, his pistol was strapped around his waist, and he had a machine gun in his hand, but I don't remember seeing the machine gun when he came back with El Jefe.

A salty stream of sweat stings my eyes. I'm almost out of breath, and I know Estéban can't run much further. He's slowing me down, but I can't leave him here. If I do, they'll kill him, and without him, I don't know where I'm going.

"*Vámonos*," I remind him, again. "We're almost there."

It seems like we've been running forever when I catch a glimpse of blue sky. We're near the road, but what if one of the commandos is there, waiting for us? What if the guard in the tower across the road knows we've escaped? Even if we make it to the car and drive away, there could be another jungle trail further up the road where they could stop us or shoot us on sight.

Estéban's car is just as we left it. I jump in the front passenger seat and give Estéban the keys. He's sputtering blood and having trouble catching his breath, and he's shaking and having a hard time getting the key in the ignition. The key finally makes the connection. The engine starts, and Estéban puts it in gear and pulls away.

Ahead of us, the jungle grows closer to the road than it did behind us, and the treetops curve into an overhead arch like the trees that line the driveway of my Spy House on the Hill. I scan both sides of the road, searching for movement of any kind, for someone coming out of the jungle. I turn to check the view out of the rear window, but the dust from our tires has made the countryside opaque.

"Don't stop!" I tell Estéban. "No matter what!"

The road climbs upward and then dips back down. Through the side windows, I see nothing but jungle on both sides. There are no signs of the Guatemalan military commandos. By now someone must be coming after us, if for no other reason than to avenge what I did to Romeo, but will they come out of the jungle in front of us, or maybe gain on us from behind? I wonder if they'll fire at us with their machine guns. If their bullets will hit their mark.

Once again the road turns upward, but Estéban's taxi doesn't have the horsepower to go any faster. We crest the hill and I look out of the left rear passenger window in time to see a flash of red in the fields below. Hundreds, maybe thousands of red blooms. They're poppies. The poppies in Hell. And as suddenly as they appeared, they vanish from sight.

CHAPTER THIRTY-SIX

WE DRIVE IN SILENCE THROUGH GREEN MOUNTAINS shrouded in dense rainforests and thick jungles, and I'm unable to think about anything before the harbingers of Hell: the shallow graves along the side of the road. Romeo's hungry hands all over my breasts. His gluttonous fingers, like sharks in a feeding frenzy, tearing chunks of flesh from my hips as they ripped off my jeans.

I look over at Estéban. His lips are pressed together like a woman who's blotting her lipstick, and I can tell he's trying to make his lower lip stop bleeding. He's leaning forward in the driver's seat. His shoulders are hunched up around his neck, and his grip on the steering wheel tells me we're not far enough away to feel safe.

We haven't seen a farm or a village, not even another car, and with each passing minute, the threat of Romeo and his revenge looms larger than it did before. Estéban and I haven't spoken a word to one another, but I know we're both expecting the commandos any second now. We're rooted in fear and an open-ended dread that has no time limit.

My wrist is still bleeding, and I'm clutching Romeo's pistol. I'm not afraid of guns. I'm a Texas girl who goes varmint-busting with the guys, looking for armadillos in the middle of the night, and I wasn't afraid to pull a gun on the men who broke into my house. An armadillo is a long way from a living breathing man, but if it's them or me, I'll go down fighting. It will be a far better option than letting them do what they want with me and leaving what's left to rot on the jungle floor or adding me to the line of shallow graves along the road.

We've been driving through a relentless sameness, mile after mile of jungle on both sides of the road. I've learned what few outsiders know: I've seen what lies behind the green curtain, and the Wizard is not some benevolent being who dispenses courage and words of wisdom. He's the devil incarnate, a barbaric beast who grows poppies and turns them into poverty, misery, and death. Today I was taken, not to seek guidance from the Wizard, but to meet death, and my gut tells me that behind these jungle walls, there are more ancient cities ruled by other machine gun-toting death gods of the underworld.

My body pulsates as though someone's beating it like they would a drum, and with each opening and closing of my heart valve, it reverberates with my every fear. My thoughts haven't strayed more than a few seconds away from Romeo. I hope he never recovers the full function of his testicles and his prize penis, the one he uses as a weapon, and I hope he remembers me with excruciating pain every time it gets excited. Every. Single. Fucking. Time. In the future, when I relive his savage attack, I will imagine I shoved his pistol up his ass and pulled the trigger.

Each time Estéban slows down for a dip in the road, the breeze stops, and the humidity wraps around me as though someone is closing the lid on my coffin. The humidity transports me back to the jungle, and I feel trapped like an insect caught in the powerful web of its jailer.

What if the spider knows exactly where I am on his ever-widening web of evil? What if he lets me get far enough away to think I'm safe and then, in a moment of surprise, pounces and pierces me with his venom?

Up ahead, there are a group of people gathered on the side of the road. I start to raise Romeo's gun, but Estéban motions for me to put it down.

"The bus," he nods. "*Aqui.*"

The bus to Tikal. I never thought we'd make it this far. There isn't a sign or a building, only a place on the side of the road where everyone knows to wait.

Estéban pulls over and turns off the ignition. We sit in silence. Neither one of us leans back in our seats with sighs of relief, and it goes unsaid, but we're afraid to look at one another for fear we'll both fall apart.

In a little while, a yellow school bus passes us and comes to a full stop next to the people gathered beside the road. The brakes sound like bedsprings and squealing pigs, and they remind me of another school bus. One full of music and smiling children. It was only this morning I'd boarded the bus in Belize City, but I'm no longer the same woman. I doubt I will meet her again.

As the people begin boarding the bus, Estéban gets out of the car and retrieves my bags from the back seat. He nods at the gun in my hand and pauses before he opens my door. It's his way of telling me to let go of Romeo's pistol. I know I shouldn't take it with me, but if the spider snatches me again, he won't let me escape a second time. Like it's a hot coal from the fires of Hell, I drop the gun on the floorboard.

Estéban sets my bags down next to the bus's big rear tires. A man in a green soccer shirt is hoisting large sacks of flour onto the roof. This time, there are no chickens. No guitar. Everyone seems to be going about their day as though nothing's out of the ordinary. I want to ask them if they know what's hiding back there in the jungle. They must know! They live here! How can they not know? Even if they lack the financial means to leave, where do they get the strength to stay?

Estéban's lip is swollen, but it's stopped bleeding and he reaches out and touches my arm. I had ahold of his hand the entire time we were running through the jungle, but this is the first time he's touched me.

"*Señora.*" He looks at the ground and swallows hard and starts shaking his head back and forth. "Miss Brenda . . . *Lo siento* . . . I sorry." I want to remember the way he says my name. The lyrical way he rolls the *r* after the *b*. "*Mees Brain-da.*"

He steps back when I reach out to hug him. He doesn't have to say it, but I know he's embarrassed, afraid of letting go and not being able to pull himself together in such a public place. It's not something men in his culture do, plus to the outside world, Estéban and I don't know one another well enough to have such an emotional goodbye.

His back is to the bus when he finally leans into my shoulder with his head down, like a child leaning into their mother for comfort and protection. We have swallowed our words and now, with seconds left before we never see one another again . . . the moment is too much.

The man securing sacks and cardboard boxes to the roof and the passengers getting onboard are oblivious to the unlikely pair behind the bus. As I pull him toward me, I can feel him crying. His hair smells like woodsmoke, and I notice how much shorter he is than me.

Once again, I have role-reversed. This time with a stranger in another country, and yet he knows me better than my mother ever could. Once again, I'm the one with the strength. I've been the parent instead of the child. The caretaker instead of the wife. The one who protected them at all costs. I've learned not to get too excited or too hopeful, too down or too afraid . . . and that tears won't change a thing.

How do I say goodbye to this man who's walked through Hell with me? Literally. Through Infierno. We've known one another only since this morning, but our experience has forged a bond stronger than blood. Neither one of us will ever forget the other or what happened this day. Our memories will stay hidden below the surface of our skin where the least little thing, or maybe nothing at all, will erupt and turn them into nightmares.

I place my hands on his shoulders and look at him, and in my most convincing voice, I say, "Estéban. We're going to be okay. We're safe." I fear my words sound hollow. Like the perfunctory "Have a nice day" when the store clerk hands you the groceries, but most of all, I have no idea if Estéban and his family will be safe. What if some of the soldiers know him or his family and seek him out as payback for what I did to Romeo?

I pick up my bags, and without turning around to look at him, I board the bus and walk down the aisle, past the other passengers, until I reach the last row of seats in the back. Estéban is standing beside his red-and-white taxi, and I'm struck by how much older he looks than he did this morning. Too old to be raising young children. We hold up our hands at the same time, not in a wave, but more of a pledge of allegiance to one another and to survivorship.

The bus lurches forward and throws me off-balance, and for a second I'm ready to run. Instead I grab ahold of the seat and slide into the empty bench. My bags are on the seat next to me but I don't remember putting them there, and my passport is still tucked into the waistband of my jeans. I open the small blue book and stare at the photo.

My hair was longer then, and I had a smile on my face like I was looking forward to wherever my blue book and my next adventure took me. I remember the woman in the photograph. Even then she was hiding secrets.

Outside, the countryside shifts from jungle to a forest of ferns. Majestic mahogany trees flash past the window as I replay the same horror movie again in my mind. I can see it and smell it. Onions, cigarettes, and the wet stench of dead things. Except for my bloody wrist, the cut on the palm of my hand, and the raw gashes over my hipbones, physically I'm okay, but mentally I'm unable to fast-forward to the end of the film. I don't know what safe looks like, and yet I'd used the same word with Estéban. "We're going to be okay. We're safe." What a joke!

It feels like the big black ants from the jungle are crawling up my legs. I lift my feet off the floorboard and lean down to brush them off, but there's nothing there.

I'm still here. Everything will be okay. Maybe if I say it enough times, I'll begin to believe it, but how do I get past the gun in my back and Romeo's penis? If I could have, I would've twisted it off and left it for the ants on the jungle floor.

I'm still here. I'm okay. I want someone to put their arms around me and say these words back to me, but there's no one to do that but me. No one did that when I was a child taking care of Mother or when the men broke into my home and rifled through the things in my closet.

I try focusing on the other people on the bus, a very different group from the ones I left Belize with this morning. And that's all it takes. Once again, I'm replaying the same horror movie. I stop and try to concentrate on the other passengers; this time I see them with fresh eyes. They are quiet, with no outward signs of happiness or humor. They look defeated and wary. Perhaps it comes from fear, from living in a country where soldiers can come into your village and kill you and steal your children, and you never see them again. I feel for them because I know what it's like to live in fear.

There's a woman, three rows up on the other side of the aisle. Perhaps her son or grandson is one of the boys in the shallow graves. Like the rest of the people aboard, her expression is flat, with no outward sign of wonderment or joy. Maybe her son, her brother, or her husband is one of the commandos. How do they live amid such evil? Do they live with the fear their family may be next to lose a loved one?

My head throbs and the middle of my back hurts. I reach around and feel a knot that wasn't there this morning. It's sore, and I remember falling backward and hitting something hard. Maybe one of the big stones from the vine-covered pyramid. Then Romeo was on top of me. His eyes were wild and crazed until I touched him. Then they rolled back in his head, and I heard him gasp.

Please! Make it stop!

CHAPTER THIRTY-SEVEN

THE BUS HAS SLOWED DOWN, AND OUTSIDE THREE women are washing their laundry in the river, kneading their clothes against big smooth boulders like women have done here for centuries. One has a small toddler strapped to her back with a red *rebozo*, an oversized scarf that's draped around one shoulder and tied in the front. Their faces resemble those of the passengers on the bus—people who are resigned to their lives and their circumstances.

In another minute, the bus's squealing brakes jolt me back to the present. I've lost track of how long it's been since I said goodbye to Estéban. What if the commandos have stopped the bus? What if they're doing a passenger check, looking for me? I slouch down in the seat and tuck my head into my chest.

I hear the other passengers getting off, and I look up long enough to see some of them taking their belongings while others are leaving theirs on the seats. When everyone has gotten off, the driver walks partway down the aisle and signals to me.

What if the commandos are waiting outside for me? My hands are sweaty. *I can't go with them. It's better if they shoot me here than take me with them.*

"*Comer?*" The driver motions like he is bringing food to his mouth. "*Quieres de comida?*"

The bus driver appears to have no other agenda than to tell me we've stopped for food. Relief washes over me like the incoming tides of the ocean. Food would be good. Maybe it will quell the vise-grip headache that's been squeezing both sides of my skull. I stand up in the aisle, but my legs are wobbly and unsteady. My fight-or-flight energy is tapped out.

Outside on the side of the road, a woman is filling *empanadas al minutos,* corn tortillas with mashed potatoes and carrots. She seals the edges with her fingers and then hands them to her husband, who cooks them over a small iron grate. I get in line behind the other passengers, and when it's my turn, I buy one of the empanadas, a hard-boiled egg, and a soft drink served in a *plastico*—a baggie with a straw inserted in the top.

My T-shirt and jeans are stippled with dirt and blood, mine and Estéban's, and I've used them to wipe Romeo's penis and his testicles off my hands. I make one last pass with my hands across the shoulders of my shirt, the only places I haven't used.

With one long gulp, I drink the contents of the plastico, then set it on the table and buy another. I swallow the hard-boiled egg and the empanada, barely stopping to register the hot sauce made from small peppers that resemble tiny, pale, green rosebuds. They have just enough fire and kick to center me. The rest stop is brief, and I'm grateful for the distraction and the food and something to drink.

From the bus window next to me, I can tell the terrain outside is becoming more mountainous. I see what looks like schefflera plants the size of three-story buildings with leaves that are green on one side and the color of brushed aluminum on the other. There are bromeliads the size of big bass drums, and everywhere there's a sweet smell that reminds me of the cottonwood trees in Texas.

Occasionally, I catch a glimpse in the distance of what looks like an unexcavated Maya ruin on top of a mountain. One peak, in particular, rises above the tree line, and I imagine underneath the heavy green thicket is a crumbling observatory that points toward the heavens. Maybe it was where the ancient Maya looked for guidance and tracked summer solstices in the night sky.

I doubt the ancient Maya would be shocked about what happened to me today. The carvings on their pyramids and stela stones depict kings, wearing magnificent breastplates and Quetzalcoatl-feathered headdresses, looking on as young virgins are sacrificed to the Sun God. I'm not a young virgin, but I was almost sacrificed to a warrior's carnal cravings and a long heritage that says men can do whatever they want to a woman.

Now and then, a break in the jungle foliage reveals a view of the horizon and the setting sun. I watch as the sky changes from dusty shades of pale pink and gold to a fusion of tangerine, violet, and indigo.

The bus has come to a complete stop, and when the rest of the passengers depart, the driver tells me this is Tikal. It's the reason I came to Guatemala in the first place. Until this moment, I'd forgotten about Tikal.

The driver points to a one-story structure on the other side of the road. "Hotel . . . *es muy bueno.*"

It's late, and I don't see another alternative. I thank him, and take his suggestion, and check into the small hotel. My room is $8 US. Basic but clean.

I drop my bags on the single bed next to an oversized pump-action container of bug spray. The bed is the only piece of furniture in the room, and it appears to have been made from something resembling Tinkertoys. On the wall over the bed hangs a framed color page from a magazine, a picture of a snow-covered Swiss chalet. Next to it, a pair of exposed wires protrude from a peach wall, and a bottle opener is screwed into the nearby doorframe. The room has one small window covered in a flowered oilcloth and a forty-watt bare bulb hangs from a ceiling that's been painted electric blue.

I'm dirty, and I smell bad, and my clothes, especially my bra and panties, have become depositories for fear and sweat. The tiny bathroom has a roll of grayish-green toilet tissue with a coarse muslin texture that feels like something used to wrap mummies in ancient Egypt, but there are no towels and no soap. I want a shower. I want to scrub my hands and breasts and any part of me Romeo touched. I want to wash him and the jungle and the horrors of the day down the drain as though none of it happened.

I tuck some money into the back pocket of my jeans, then step into the hallway and lock the door behind me. Except for me, the hotel appears to be deserted, but on the other side of the small courtyard, I see an open kitchen where a young woman is mopping the floor.

"*Perdóneme . . . Tienes jabón?*" I ask for soap, but I don't know the Spanish word for *towel* so in English I say, "Soap and a towel?"

She points to a vibrant blue table the same color as the ceiling in my room. On top is a plastic bottle of liquid dish soap and a small stack of neatly folded hand towels. "*Tienes más grande?*" The young woman shakes her head. *No.* There aren't any larger towels.

It's dark outside, and the courtyard is alive with the sounds of the jungle at night. The birds have taken a backseat to an eerie chorus of howler monkeys that sound like a pride of angry prehistoric lions. I ask if I can get something to eat. Again, she shakes her head *no* but then gestures for me to sit down at another blue table. In a few minutes, she brings me two yellow corn tortillas on a red plastic plate.

"*Muchas gracias.*" In this part of the world, I've learned the hard way not to drink tap water or brush my teeth with anything but bottled water. "*Tienes agua en botella?*"

Once more the young woman shakes her head *no.*

"*Tienes cerveza?*" This time she nods *yes.* "*Dos cerveza, por favor.*"

When she brings the beer, I leave more than enough money to cover everything. Then I juggle the beers and the plate of tortillas, the stack of small hand towels, and the dish soap and take them back to my room.

Once inside, I lock the door behind me and drag the small bed until it's blocking the door. I know my security is only an illusion. If someone wanted to get in, the door and the Tinkertoy bed would be history, but the simple act of blocking it tells me I haven't folded inward. I haven't shut down with fear and slid off the edge into helplessness and depression like my mother did after my father died.

I step out of my clothes and push them into the corner of the bathroom floor with my foot. I want no part of them, ever again, except for my shoes. Other than a pair of black scuba fins, the Keds are the only shoes I brought with me. Parts of them are still damp from the ocean in Belize, but they're no longer white. Like my T-shirt and jeans, they're colored with vivid reminders of the day.

The water in the shower is lukewarm. I cover my body with the liquid dish soap and begin scrubbing my breasts and stomach, hard, like the women I saw washing their laundry against the rocks. I scour my skin as though I'm working to remove a garish stain from a garment or maybe the first layer of skin he touched. I scrub my hair and my scalp, pausing to see if the dirt and depravity are gone from under my fingernails.

From somewhere deep inside me a jagged cry erupts. It's

been a long time coming, and I feel it rise and mix seamlessly with the growls of the howler monkeys outside. With heaving sobs, I slide down the wall to the concrete floor, my shoulders slumped and limp like Estéban's. The water beats down on the back of my head and neck, and I watch a deluge of dish soap stream and swirl in a circular motion around the drain in the floor.

I want to go home. I want to be safe in my bed with my dog, Phydaux, the only living being who makes me feel like I'm loved unconditionally. Like an angry child making mud pies, I cry and beat the palms of my hands on the floor of the shower. Romeo, Hard-Ass, the Wiry One, and the others . . . how do I make it stop?

The wound on the inside of my wrist has opened again, and I stare at my blood as it mixes with the bubbles from the dish soap and disappears down the drain. The cut is uneven, deeper than I thought, and for the first time, I notice my arms and legs are bruised and badly scratched.

Just yesterday, I'd stood on the beach in Ambergris Caye and soaked up the sun as I sent my anger and sorrow out with the tide. I wanted to let it go. I needed to let it go. To remember only the good things about my years with Philip and to make room for a new life I hoped would be safe and happy. But just when it felt like I could move on, the tide brought back a tsunami of barbarians. I wonder if there will ever be an ocean big enough for me to cast this day away.

I'm lucky to be here, and I know there are those who've been subjected to things far worse than I have. Things I don't want to imagine. My tears are for them and me.

I let the water run down my face and merge with my tears until my sobs turn into shivers. I've run out of warm water, and I take the cold as a sign I need to pull myself together. It's not time for me to give in and let all my edges soften.

The small stack of thin hand towels is barely enough to dry all of me. I run a comb through my wet hair and pull some Band-Aids and a small bottle of Listerine from my bag. The brown antiseptic liquid burns my wrist and hand, and the raw places on my hips. In the car with Estéban, I had no choice but to let my wrist bleed and, on the bus, I'd held it tight with the thumb of my other hand. At some point my wrist will stop bleeding, and the bruises will fade, but it's the places I can't see that will be the hardest to heal. The ones that hurt the most.

I wrap myself in a short black-and-white kimono and sit on the edge of the bed. The corn tortillas are cold and dry, and I wash each swallow down with the first bottle of beer. The second bottle I guzzle, hoping it will relax me enough to let me sleep.

The room is too warm for a top sheet, but I pull it up under my chin because it makes me feel like there's at least a small protective barrier between me and those who would do me harm. Like the bed in front of the door, it's another psychological ploy I use to tell myself I'll be all right. That I'm safe.

As I lie in the dark and listen to my breathing and the sounds of the jungle, it occurs to me Romeo never uttered a word. Just a gasp and a moan of pleasure followed by a low painful howl. My thoughts are in free fall. Hard-Ass's cold eyes and the chain of black ants. The barrel of the machine gun in my back and Romeo. It always comes back to Romeo, starting at the car when his fingers traced an invisible pattern on my arm.

Tears roll down the sides of my face, into my ears. I should have died today or worse. Why didn't I? I've been surviving something since the day I was born and wasn't expected to live. Even as a little girl, when I needed someone, I swallowed my fears, or maybe they were Mother's. I didn't wait for a comforting shoulder, and I showed up for myself when I mothered my mother. When Philip tried to kill me, and I blindly jumped out of a second-story window.

How will I ever acknowledge what happened today with anyone but Estéban? I've already swallowed and pushed so many colossal secrets aside. Things I can't share with anyone. How do I make room for one more?

I can see Estéban's face as the bus pulled away and left him standing there. Small, scared, and shell-shocked. I worry he'll blame himself, but he's a good man who thought they'd let us through. How am I going to live without knowing what happened to him?

We will never see one another again, but we're embedded in one another as surely as if we shared the same DNA. On the outside, we're from different cultures. But inside, we're family.

CHAPTER THIRTY-EIGHT

IT'S DAYLIGHT. I HAVEN'T GOTTEN OUT OF BED, BUT ALREADY I'm tired. At some point I must have given in to exhaustion and drifted off to sleep. The Band-Aids on my wrist have come loose. The sheets are stained with my blood, and I'm still covered with the reality of yesterday.

I get up and put new Band-Aids on my wrist, then pull a fresh T-shirt and a pair of khaki pants from my bag. The pants are lightweight and will ride better against the raw spots on my hips. Now that I'm up and moving, I'm aware that every part of my body hurts.

The man at the front desk is the same person who checked me in last night. He tells me the bus to Guatemala City won't be here until noon, but if I want to see Tikal, his father can drive me there, wait for me, and then bring me back in time to catch the bus. Part of me wants to stay in my room until the bus leaves for Guatemala City and the airport there, but if I did, I'd be letting my fears define me. For a little while longer, I will pretend to be afraid of nothing and no one.

The man behind the desk senses I'm having a problem with his suggestion, and he assures me they regularly provide this service to their guests. He proudly tells me he's the owner of the hotel. It has six rooms, and the archaeologists and a film crew stayed there while they were excavating Tikal.

No matter what I do, this will be a defining moment for me. In the past, I've ignored my feelings and pretended to be all right. Regardless of what I decide, I won't allow myself to sit in the dark with the shades pulled. Staying holed up isn't living. It's going through the motions, marking time until I die. My feelings about seeing Tikal have changed, and I no longer want to go, but it's something I must do. If not, I will have gone to Hell and back for nothing.

I tell the hotel owner I'd appreciate it if his father would drive me to Tikal and wait for me, and then bring me back in time to catch my bus.

When we arrive at Tikal it's not even eight in the morning, but the temperature and the humidity have shackled me with the same claustrophobic feeling that surrounded me yesterday: like someone's closing the lid on my coffin. I rub my thumb across the fresh set of Band-Aids on my wrist and remind myself that yesterday was a fluke. The odds of it happening again are virtually impossible.

I force myself to take a step into the jungle, followed by another and another, swatting at the legions of mosquitos as I go. With each stride, I replay everything about the commandos who boxed me in with their weapons and forced me into the jungle. They're part of the film that won't stop playing in my head.

Just like yesterday, the jungle is filled with the warning cries of birds and monkeys, but today, there's a new sound. Hordes of cicadas are cracking and popping their wings, and they've joined the existing chorus to make me feel like an unwelcome outsider.

Up ahead, several tree roots resemble grotesque oversized snakes, writhing and twisting their way across the jungle floor while broadleaf palms and a string of hot pink orchids vie for the same narrow rays of the sun. Everywhere I note delicate moss and bird's-nest ferns that have exploded from the trunks of the towering trees.

Fanning out from the edge of the jungle, Tikal's main plaza stretches before me, and it's flanked on either side by towering temples. The only other people here are four young men who're descending the steps of one of the temples. They look like they could be Americans, but as they get closer, I realize they're speaking French.

I did well in my high school French classes. "*Bonjour*," I say.

One of them offers me a half-hearted "*Bonjour*" as he and his friends keep walking past me, engrossed in their conversation.

I don't know what I expected. Perhaps they would stop, and we would exchange bits of travel information like tourists sometimes do when they're off the beaten path. I wanted a connection with home, but more than that, I wanted to know if they'd traveled down the road to Hell, and if so, had they been stopped by the military commandos?

Except for me, the main plaza is now empty. Since the first time I saw Tulum, I've dreamed of having another Maya ruin to myself, but now that I'm here, I'm fighting the overwhelming urge to run. The pyramid's stone steps are tall and narrow, not deep enough for my foot to fit without my heels hanging off the back of each step. I force myself to take the first step and then another. My balance is unsteady, and I feel exposed and defenseless.

When I get a third of the way to the top, I can see over the surrounding trees. In every direction, there's nothing but miles of thick jungle, and hidden inside are a thousand varieties of life, each teeming with the same primal quest for survival. The floppy valve in my heart has started fluttering again, and I'm feeling trapped, caged by unseen predators waiting to swoop in and take me prisoner. I'm exposed, too exposed. I need to get down.

I sidestep my way down the pyramid with my back hand on the step behind me, so I won't lean too far forward and lose my balance and fall. By the time I reach the bottom steps, my arms and legs are shaking, and just like it did last night in the shower, my body crumples and folds in on itself. I'm a marionette that's lost its strings—and the one who pulls them—and the tears I've worked so hard to hold back have once again torn down my defenses.

I sink to my knees and cry for what happened yesterday, together with every tear I've ever wanted to shed but couldn't. I cry for the Philip I lost long before he died of cancer and for the terrified woman who hid in the bushes behind the barn. I cry for the arm's length father and the mother who was really the child. My eyes are drowning in tears, but they don't prevent me from seeing each of the women I've been and the pain I've stuffed inside and haven't allowed myself to feel.

Once again, the flying insects have found me. They're relentless, like all the feelings I've bottled up inside me. It occurs to me the people I cry for are just like me. Human and flawed. Maybe it was me who failed them, but none of us did it deliberately.

On the other side of the jungle, past the shrieks and howls and the multitudes of mosquitos, the driver from the small hotel is waiting for me. But this time, I won't pretend I'm fine and everything is all right. I get to my feet and start running, past the orchids and the snaky tree roots. I will run from this place as fast as I can.

CHAPTER THIRTY-NINE

THE BUS TO GUATEMALA CITY HAS PULLED AWAY FROM the hotel and stopped a short distance down the road in front of a small cinder-block building with a pale blue door. It's a *comedor y hospedaje*, a communal place where workers and *campesinos* can drink a few beers, get something to eat, and have a place to sleep for the night. I've seen the inside of another similar place, so I don't need to see this one to imagine there might be tables on one side and hammocks hanging from the ceiling on the other. The food is good and cheap. Simple food like *frijoles* and *arroz*, *carne adovada*, *huevos con chorizo*, tortillas, and cold cerveza. But the one thing I couldn't have imagined is the name on the front of the building.

Hand-lettered in black paint are the words, *Comedor Y Hospedaje Brenda*. I am dumbstruck by the name.

A man dressed in work clothes has boarded the bus, and he's struggling to get a large wooden box down the aisle. Before the driver closes the door and pulls away, I grab the camera from my bag in time to take a picture before the building fades from view. *Comedor Y Hospedaje Brenda*. It is the only photograph I've taken since I left Ambergris Caye yesterday morning.

I've never met another woman named Brenda, and there

aren't many businesses in this part of the world owned by or named after women. Part of me believes the name on the building was an apparition, like when people in the desert need water and think they see a watering hole that turns out to be nothing more than an illusion of water. A mirage. Perhaps I'm like the people in the desert, but instead of water, I need comfort and reassurance. Reassurance I'll make it to the airport in Guatemala City. Perhaps the place of hospitality with my name on it was nothing more than an illusion. A mirage my mind created to comfort me.

Most of the women in this part of the world are without a voice, and I can identify with them because somewhere along the line, I lost mine. Without meeting her, I know the Brenda who owns the *hospedaje* is strong and determined. I shudder to think of the circumstances and the men she may have survived, and it strikes me that we're more alike than either one of us could imagine. I like her already. Like me, she knows how to be there for herself when no one else is there for her.

The gash on my wrist has opened and it's bleeding again— perhaps from the strain of lifting my bags onto the bus. I search my canvas duffle bag until I locate the small bottle of Listerine and then pour a few drops on my wrist. I'm out of Band-Aids, but I find a scarf in the bottom of my bag and wrap it tightly around the cut.

I stare at the trees outside the window until they become an out-of-focus wall of seamless green foliage. What started as the first carefree week I can remember in a long time has me thinking about the men I've survived. How ironic: A little more than twenty-four hours ago I'd arrived at a good place. I'd shed some of the dark days with Philip and left them in the ocean as I snorkeled the colorful reefs of Ambergris Caye.

My favorite photograph of Philip was taken there. He's

laughing and looking at a multicolored parrot perched on his hand. I saw Philip everywhere I went on the island, and I took comfort because that was the Philip I loved. The one before everything changed. Now those memories, along with the ones of my bus ride with the little girls and their meat tacos, Mr. Rooster, and Bobby Vinton, have been seized at gunpoint. I've lived a lifetime in one day, and now a Brenda I've never met has inspired me to believe another lifetime awaits me.

I want to believe the last words I said to Estéban are true: "We're going to be okay. We're safe." Because if they are, they'll be more valuable than all the gold the ancient Maya ground into dust and blew onto their bodies with long hollow canes.

Since the day I was born, I've made it through one trauma after another, and I've survived them by more than *pretending* to be afraid of nothing and no one. I won't let yesterday cripple me. I have a choice to make, and I'm choosing to move forward because the other alternatives frighten me. I've seen how they turned out for Mother and Philip.

Outside the window, the jungle and the mountain forest have given way to a small house on a tiny postcard of land. The owners have planted rows and rows of corn, and there are chickens and a rooster in the yard. The people who live there have made the most of what they have. Like them, I will be the result of the seeds I sow and how I choose to deal with what life puts in my path today, yesterday, and tomorrow.

Life is a gift, and sometimes it hangs in the balance, waiting while medicine and miracles intercede and breathe new strength into our bodies. Other times, life demands nothing more from us than to take it in and learn from it. With each new experience, good and bad, we can decide to emerge on the other side as an altered version of ourselves, a stronger, better self. I will go home and create a new beginning. One without

Philip, the men who broke into my home, and the soldiers from *Infierno*.

With each beat of my heart, I tell myself I'll be surrounded by colors and images that strengthen and soothe me, and I will nourish my soul as I chart a new course. Maybe I'll take one step forward and a dozen steps back, but I'll keep going. I won't let anything hold me hostage, and I will never again let myself be subservient to someone else's voice.

I close my eyes and focus on the rhythmic sound of the wheels on the road. I breathe in the air from the open window and imagine a vision of my younger self. The young woman who first became enchanted with Tulum. Before I knew about cocaine in the dungeon and the poppies in Hell, Tulum resonated with me on a level I could never put into words. When I think about Tulum, it's almost like being in a state of meditative prayer, but in this moment, I've lost sight of how to reclaim the sense of peace and well-being I had when I was there.

Once again I close my eyes and rest my head on the seatback behind me and imagine myself sitting on the edge of the Temple of the Wind God. There's no one there but me. The sea below is calm. The sky is clear, and I can feel the warmth of the sun on my face. I say the name, Sian Ka'an, the place where the sky was born, over and over like a mantra. It has an exotic cadence to it, and phonetically, I break it down and put the accent on the first two letters of each word the way the Maya did.

Shhh makes me think of a loving mother who puts her fingers to her lips to calm her crying child. "*Shhh*. Everything will be all right." *Shhh-an. Ka* sounds like the beginning of the word calm. *Ka-an. Shhh-an Ka-an.* Sian Ka'an. From now on this will be the place in my mind where I go to feel safe and calm.

Like the first time I was there, I can feel Tulum's energy as it vibrates in waves and then rises and joins forces with the sky, just as it did when the ancient Maya believed it was the place where the sky was born. I imagine the energy there wraps around me like a powerful protective cloak, and I have the power to come and go whenever I want.

I gather my strength, and stand on the top of the temple, and raise my arms toward the sky. A breeze comes in from the ocean, and I see myself ascending upward like one of the great birds of Sian Ka'an. I see Itzamná, the sky god, and the rain god, Chac, together with the moon, the stars, and all the fish below. The bad things that have happened to me and the thoughts and patterns that don't serve me well . . . I shake them off and watch them drop into the depths of the dark blue sea.

CHAPTER FORTY-ONE

FOR ALL OF MY BIG SELF-TALK ON THE BUS ABOUT accessing my strength, Tulum's powerful cloak has dropped from my shoulders and left me feeling naked and afraid. Even before I walked through the doors of the airport in Guatemala City, I was terrified my passport would be red-flagged. Romeo and the other commandos know my name, and I fear there will be men in camouflage uniforms, carrying machine guns, who will pull me aside and tell me I can't leave the country.

I draw on my well-honed skills at pretending everything's all right and inquire at the ticket counter about available flights to San Antonio, today.

The agent at the desk tells me, "If we hurry, I think we can get you on the last flight to Houston with a connecting flight to San Antonio. Will that work?"

I force a smile and try not to sound desperate. "That would be great. Thank you." The agent doesn't know it, but I would buy a ticket to almost anywhere as long as I can leave Guatemala, now.

With my ticket in hand, I follow the signs toward the gate and do my best to blend in with the other passengers who look like they're on their way home from vacation. When I reach the gate, I learn my flight has finished boarding, and they're about to close the door to the aircraft. A customs officer is standing next to the gate attendant, and like yesterday in the jungle, my heart starts beating out of rhythm. First a series of fast, irregular beats followed by enough missed beats to make me wonder if my heart will stop altogether.

I hold out my boarding pass and my passport and concentrate on my breathing. Regular breaths in and out. Nothing too rapid or too shallow. I'm scared of doing anything that will draw attention to myself or keep me from getting on the plane.

The man at the gate signals the flight attendant in the doorway of the plane to wait while the customs officer examines my documents. He looks at my passport photo, and just like the commando did yesterday in the jungle, he looks at me. After what seems like an eternity of missed heartbeats, he hands it back to me and gives my boarding pass to the gate attendant who waves me on through.

My mouth is dry and my legs are unsteady, but I force myself to walk, not run, down the boarding ramp to the plane. I find my seat, put my canvas bag in the overhead compartment and store my camera case under my feet, all while looking out the windows for signs they're coming for me.

In a few minutes the doors close and the plane taxis down the runway. It gathers speed as it goes, and then lifts off, but I can't allow myself to relax because I have one more hurdle to conquer. I have to clear US Customs in Houston. What if my name is on a list there, and I'm not allowed to enter the United States? What if they send me back to Guatemala?

It's not until I drive through the gate, up the hill and under the arched green porte cochere to the Spy House that I grant myself permission to feel safe. How ironic to feel safe in the same house where the fairy tale turned into a nightmare. Where I tasked myself with holding everything together, trying to ignore my feelings and rehabilitate a husband who wobbled back and forth on the edge of drug-induced insanity. This time, I promise myself, living here will be different. I will be different.

PART THREE

FINDING MY VOICE

"I don't think you can come into your wisdom until
you have made mistakes on your own skin and felt
them in reality of your own life."

—ELIZABETH GILBERT

CHAPTER FORTY-ONE

"I DON'T FEEL SORRY FOR YOU AT ALL." JESSE, THE MAN I began seeing six months after Philip died, is standing in the middle of my living room. The look on his face is void of any sympathy for what I escaped three days before. "What did you think was going to happen to you, traveling in that part of the world by yourself?"

Jesse's words are cold and callous, and I feel as though I've been tossed aside on a trash heap along with the other people who've been discarded and whose emotions don't matter to anyone. Once again, I've been demolished by a storm I didn't see coming, cast adrift on an uninhabited island with no emergency rescue flares and no one who would see them. His words reverberate in the dark of my throat like the evil that grows and flows from the wicked, unimaginable things in the jungle.

Maybe this is how countless other women feel who've been told the sexual assault committed against them was their fault. *You shouldn't have been there in the first place. You shouldn't have been dressed that way. You were asking for it.* And what if he's right? What if I'd been reckless and impulsive to venture into a country alone, to a place I knew nothing about?

I hold my breath and bite down, hard, on my emotions. This is not the reaction I expected. *You're safe now* was the response I needed. *I've got you.* But then maybe I shouldn't be too surprised.

Jesse and I have never fooled ourselves into believing ours is a forever relationship. He isn't Mr. Right, and I'm not "the one." We're two people who are "right now," and that's okay, but now I'm wondering what I'm doing with him. I rushed into this relationship without really knowing him.

At first glance, Jesse checked all the boxes: tall and boyishly handsome with salt-and-pepper hair—an electrical engineer who worked for Datapoint in the early days when it was known as Computer Terminal Corporation. We know many of the same people, but we'd never had a conversation until I ran into him after Philip died.

In the beginning, Jesse was fun and I was desperate to feel normal. He was laid back and great at keeping me in the here and now. Our relationship was good therapy until he started reverting to his old ways—ones I knew nothing about, like his all-consuming narcissism. Then there's the little matter of his being a womanizer.

It doesn't matter whether a woman's fat or skinny, attractive or homely. When a female walks by, Jesse stops what he's doing and tracks her every move as though his eyes are implanted in a robotic bobblehead doll. Once he left me standing on a curb while he ran across a parking lot and pressed his face against a restaurant window so he could continue staring at an obese woman in a black and white polka-dot dress.

I want a man who values me, but that's a box Jesse doesn't check. I no longer know what a loving, caring relationship should feel like. Maybe I've never known. I know only the ones that leave me feeling raw and vulnerable and abandoned. I don't know another person who carries the same kind of scars I bear. How can I possibly explain what I've witnessed and lived through to people who have no idea these things even exist?

From my seat in the living room I watch Jesse walk away, and instinctively I do what I've done since childhood. I swallow my feelings. That horrific day in the jungle will become one more thing I bury deep inside for fear others will judge me the way Jesse judged me.

Just as I've done with Philip, I've internalized what happened in Guatemala. During the day, I bury it and pretend I've lived what most people call *a normal life*. I fix dinner, do laundry, and I'm learning how to use an Apple Macintosh computer. But at night, what happened in the jungle guts my ability to sleep. When I turn off the lights, unimaginable images run past me in the dark, flashes of hidden truths where all my secrets come together in a kaleidoscope of terror. Some nights I find myself consumed with reliving them as though they're happening in real time, until I'm engulfed in a river of quiet tears.

Other nights I zero in on the details like the black sword on the patch stitched onto Romeo's uniform, or I think about the way his eyes rolled back in his head when my hand brushed against his penis. Sometimes, when I do get to sleep, I dream of being overtaken by the jungle, imprisoned by the oversized roots of the giant ficus trees. Layers and layers of rotted trees have fallen on top of me, and they're covered in the same thick woody vines that obscure the Maya pyramids. No one can hear my screams.

I've tried late-night television, herbal tea, a shower, even a warm glass of milk, but sleep doesn't come easily, and Jesse doesn't want to hear about Guatemala. He draws strength from beating me down at every opportunity with cruel one-liners like, "You're too stupid to know when you're in trouble." His remarks leave me feeling like I've been run over by an asphalt roller.

CHAPTER FORTY-TWO

ON THE SURFACE JESSE COMES ACROSS AS A FRIENDLY guy who likes everyone, but underneath he's a seething mass of class consciousness and anger. He hates anyone he perceives as rich, especially the people who run the tech company he works for, and the guy who owned the condo he used to rent.

"People like that take advantage of people like me," he tells me, ignoring the fact that he drives a Porsche, albeit an old one, and spends all his money on the latest computers and high-tech gadgets, along with toys like golf clubs and windsurfing boards. He pauses to look at me, and then sneers, "You look rich."

"It's just blue jeans and a white shirt."

"Well, you make them look rich!" His tone is loathsome and contemptuous. "It's your fault I didn't finish my work last night. I told you I needed to be home early." The guy who chooses to prioritize windsurfing and golf and doesn't start work-related projects until the day before they're due has made his failure my fault.

"We've been through this, Jesse. The restaurant was busy, and the waiter was slow. It wasn't anyone's fault."

It's long past time to break it off with him. If I don't, he'll be the second man I've stayed with when I knew I shouldn't. But breaking it off won't be easy; he's living in my house.

"Our relationship isn't working anymore, Jesse. I need you to move out."

"I *can't* move! I don't have any money! *You* move!" There is venom in his voice, and his eyes have narrowed into angry, glaring slits.

"This is my house. I'm not leaving."

"Then you better get used to me." He yanks a table lamp out of the electrical socket and hurls it at me. "Because I'm not leaving either!"

The lamp sails past my shoulder and gouges a large chunk of plaster out of the wall behind me while Jesse continues his verbal tirade. His violence is a trigger for all of my fears, not just Guatemala, but the night Philip choked me, and all the times I wondered if the men who broke into our house would kill us.

I grab my purse and run past him, but not before his fist lands a blow on the side of my face. My eye and cheekbone hurt, and I'm afraid of what he'll do to me, but I keep running, down the front steps to my car.

I back my car out of the garage. Jesse's followed me, and he's trying to open the driver's door, but he can't. I've locked it. He's barefoot, wearing only his briefs, and he's beating on the window next to my head.

"Open the door!"

A panicky feeling washes over me in waves. He's enraged, and I'm afraid he'll beat the shit out of me if he gets the chance. As I put the car in drive, he throws himself onto the hood. His face is inches from mine, separated by the windshield, and he's growling at me like a wild animal that's escaped from a cage, screaming for me to stop the car.

My racing experience kicks in. I accelerate and then brake hard, and the maneuver bucks him off. He lands on his feet and starts lunging toward my car, but I've accelerated down the driveway. Out of his reach. Through the rearview mirror, I catch a brief glimpse of him, standing in the driveway. Arms raised. Fists clenched.

I'm shaking, running on adrenaline, afraid to think about what he might have done to me. *What happened to the resilient woman who's already been to Hell and swore she'd never go back? How did I let myself get involved in another relationship where I made the man in my life the king at my expense?* After everything I've been through with Philip, I've repeated it with Jesse. I've conned myself into believing if I was quiet and low profile, we would stay on an even keel, and I wouldn't be lost on another man's train. It's easy to say, but I need to stop tiptoeing around a leopard that will never change his spots. The hard part is breaking old patterns and doing it.

My big mobile phone, the size of my foot, is next to me in the front passenger seat, and I dial 911 and call the police. The officer on the other end of the phone says a police car will meet me in five minutes at the Exxon station across the street from my house.

I'm angry at myself. There have been other red flags I've chosen to ignore. Jesse's been freeloading off me, plus he owes me money. I should've asked him to leave a long time ago, but I've been afraid of a confrontation or something worse.

The mobile phone rings, and it's Jesse.

"Every minute you're not here, I'm going to shoot something."

In the background I can hear Phydaux barking, followed by a gunshot, and then silence. The line goes dead. *Oh, God! Did he kill my dog?*

Like something out of *Hawaii Five-0*, three police cars have pulled into the Exxon station and surrounded my car. When they see I'm alone, they ask me to step out of the car. I tell them what happened and that Jesse's found the handgun I keep. One of the officers tells me to get in the backseat of his patrol car, and with me in the last car, all three police vehicles drive up the hill to my house.

The officers instruct me to stay put while, one by one, they fan out around the house, guns drawn. Once the house is secured, one of the officers stands at the top of my front steps and motions for me to come inside. The wreckage I can see from the front door looks like a tornado has ripped through the living room all the way to the bedroom. I was right to be afraid of Jesse.

Bullet holes mar the bedroom walls. My ficus trees have been pulled out of their pots by the roots and the pots thrown against the walls. A glass tabletop is smashed and fallen inward with shards sticking up in every direction like a dangerous game of Pick-up Sticks. In the kitchen, Jesse has ripped the cabinets off the walls with his bare hands. Cans of tomatoes and beans, spices, boxes of cereal, and broken plates are scattered across the floor, but what alarms me more than anything is the pot of freshly brewed coffee.

In the fifteen minutes since I left him standing in my driveway, Jesse unleashed his unbridled rampage. Then he got dressed and boiled water, ground fresh coffee beans, and retrieved a Chemex coffee filter from the debris on the floor and made coffee, which he's now offering to the officers as though they've stopped by for a social visit. But it's Phydaux's absence that scares me the most. I ask the officers but none of them have seen him.

I run through the main floor of the house, calling his name. There's no response. The front door's been open, probably since I fled. The thought of him running loose on busy Judson Road or IH-35 is terrifying.

I race upstairs, and by the time I reach the secret closets I can see Phydaux's paws, sticking out from under my desk. I lean down and crawl under there with him and put my head next to his. Like me, he's shaking but physically okay.

My heart feels like it's going to ricochet out of my chest. *How do I recover from this?* Not just from Jesse, but from everything? I want to feel safe and loved. There's no more room in my psyche for a narcissist or a drug addict or someone who keeps me at arms' length. I want a man who returns my love—someone who values and appreciates me—and I need the ability to recognize the difference.

To ensure that Phydaux stays safe, I close the French doors to my office.

Downstairs, Jesse is standing in the living room in handcuffs next to a police officer I haven't seen.

"I'm with the family violence intervention unit." His voice is calm, but his words pack a punch. "The next time this guy may kill you and then himself. We see it all the time."

The plain vanilla look on Jesse's face doesn't match the magnitude of the violence and destruction all around me, and the dichotomy is terrifying.

"You look like a smart lady. I hope you hear what I'm saying because you need to get this guy out of your life." The officer is articulating what I've been thinking. "We're going to take him downtown and book him."

"Then what happens?"

"He'll spend the night in jail and more than likely post bail in the morning."

"What good will a night in jail do?"

"Probably nothing."

Another officer I haven't seen steps through the front door and introduces himself as the sheriff. He looks at me as he hands the family intervention officer a piece of paper. "We ran a check on him. Did you know he's been arrested on similar charges before?"

I shake my head *no* as I grapple with the fact that I'm not the only woman he's abused.

"I suggest you get your attorney to take out a protective order against him, and if I were you, I wouldn't be here when he gets out of jail. You're too isolated up here on this hill."

At this point the idea of an angry Jesse on the loose is almost as frightening as the commandos in the jungle. I watch as one of the officers leads him out the front door and down the steps to one of the patrol cars in my driveway. When he's out of earshot I say, "What if I offer not to press charges on the condition he gets some therapy?"

"If that's what you want to do. Personally I wouldn't cut this guy any slack. I can loan out an officer to stay here for two days, but I can't have him here until tomorrow morning. After that I suggest you hire a bodyguard. In case he posts bail today, do you have someplace you can stay?"

This time it's not a law firm that suggests I need a bodyguard but the sheriff. There are too many things that have repeated themselves in my life, and this is one more I didn't see coming.

When the officers leave, I turn off the coffee and pack an overnight bag. I load Phydaux and his bowls and the bag of his food into my car, and drive to the old Sheraton Hotel on the Austin Highway. I check in under an assumed name—the maiden name of a high school girlfriend. The last time I was here was for a high school prom. Even then I'd been keeping secrets about life at home.

———

The violence intervention facility's ceilings are low, and the hallways are cold and unimaginative. Jesse's been admitted, and his psychiatrist has called and said he wants to meet with me.

"We can offer these guys some therapy while they're here, but it's been my experience they don't take it. I'd rather figure out why *you're* sick. Why you're with this guy."

His statement offends me. Sick, as in mentally sick, is when you break down and can't cope with life, but regardless of what happens to me, I keep charging. The psychiatrist doesn't know it, but I'm Ramborella. He doesn't know about Guatemala, or the other unthinkable things I've survived, or that after each one I keep on going.

"Do you know what the thousand-yard stare is?"

"No."

"In the few minutes we've been talking, you've been staring right here." He points to a spot between his eyebrows. "Soldiers who've been in battle have the thousand-yard stare. It's blank and unfocused. They're looking, but they're not really plugged in. It's a sign of too much trauma."

That's me. I have a PhD in trauma. Sometimes I catch myself looking at that exact spot on someone's face while they're talking to me and I realize I haven't been listening.

"I know a good therapist who works with abused women. If I get you an appointment, will you see her?"

A brief recognition begins to stir. One that, until now, I haven't admitted because I didn't know what an abused woman looked like. I've trained myself to let the arrows bounce off me. I've pretended I'm all right and told myself I can handle anything, but as the psychiatrist is talking, I realize I don't want to do this anymore. I don't want to choose the wrong man again, and I don't want to hide behind an assortment of fake pretenses I've lined up like freshly painted boards on a picket fence.

"Yes," I finally say. "I'll see her." I need someone who can help me with more than Jesse. Someone who can rescue the emerging butterfly that doesn't know where to land.

After four private sessions with the therapist, I've started going to her Monday night meetings for abused women, but so far I can't identify with any one of them.

I'm not an abused woman, I tell myself. *I just had a husband who got off track, then I hooked up with the boyfriend from Hell. That could happen to anyone.*

One woman in the group is a meth addict who's missing two of her teeth. Another woman seems to have a perpetual black eye and shares a trailer with her two kids and a mother-in-law she doesn't like. Then there's the attorney. The man she married is also a lawyer who physically and emotionally abuses her and just when she's had enough and decides to leave him, she changes her mind.

"I know he'll change," she keeps saying. "I just need to wait it out."

After forty-five minutes of being instructed to stand with each foot on an oversized pillow that are three feet apart, she finally speaks up. "It's a difficult balancing act to stay like this. I don't want to do this anymore."

"I'm sure you don't." It's all the therapist says to her.

And like I've been struck by a meteor, it hits me. The power is mine, not theirs. I don't have to keep doing this. I don't have to stay in these destructive relationships. I don't have to find my balance in their out of kilter world.

I've moved from a relationship with an addict to one with an abusive narcissist, and with both men, I've traded free will and common sense in return for feeling loved. But with Jesse it's not even real love. I've settled for having someone in my life, but every minute of every day has been a balancing act, like trying to stand upright on fat fluffy pillows.

If the next man in my life turns out to be controlling, disrespectful, or always puts himself first . . . color me gone!

CHAPTER FORTY-THREE

"IT'S NONE OF YOUR FUCKING BUSINESS. WHAT ELSE DO you want to know?"

The more aggressive of Advanced Tobacco Products' two co-CEOs is sitting across the table from me in his office. He's a good friend, someone I've known for years, and I didn't expect him to respond with such bully tactics to my question: *What are the plans for the company now that it's no longer manufacturing FAVOR? Now that the Feds have asked the company to voluntarily withdraw FAVOR from the marketplace.*

Removing FAVOR from the market is a big dog on the block move by the Feds and the Big Six. *They won't let you get away with it* had been our greatest fear since day one. We've always known FAVOR underscored what the government and the big tobacco companies wanted to remain hidden: Cigarettes are a drug delivery system for nicotine, the only alkaloid not classified by the DEA as a drug, and the Big Six's delivery system is killing their customers.

I'm here talking to Advanced Tobacco Products' co-CEOs because of a phone call I received earlier this morning. The man on the other end of the phone had said, "I speak for a group of unhappy shareholders. We're talking to you because you're the fattest rabbit," a term that implied I'm the single largest shareholder. The one with the most to gain or lose. "If you're confident with where the company's going then we'll feel better about our investment, but right now we don't think things are headed in the right direction."

I did more listening than talking until the caller said, "As you know, this Monday is the company's annual shareholder meeting. If you don't have anything good to tell us before then, we might take action of our own." When I asked what they had in mind he'd answered with, "Let's just say we'd rather know you're happy." I didn't ask for details, because it was clear what he meant: unless I can give them a reason not to, they are planning a takeover of the company.

A group of powerful, disgruntled shareholders is never a good thing, especially since ATP's stock is critical to my financial future. I can't afford to let them do something that might drive the stock price down any further than it's already fallen since FAVOR's no longer on the market. I'd made them promise they wouldn't do anything until after I met with the company's executives.

If the smartass co-CEO across from me responded to a shareholder the way he's talking to me . . . *It's none of your fucking business. What else do you want to know?* . . . I can see why they're having doubts.

His statement is shocking and uncalled for, but instead of raising the temperature even more, I look at the man who's been my friend for almost twenty years and say, "Surely you can tell me something."

"You're not management, and you're not a board member, which means you're not entitled to insider information."

Until Philip died I knew everything, but things are different now, and I understand the implications of "insider information." While it's a position I don't want to put either one of us in, I'm not sure whether to be alarmed or pissed off by the way he's treating me. Regardless, it's raised the stakes on my conversation with the shareholder this morning. I need time to think about things, but the clock is ticking. The shareholder meeting is six days away.

My friend Stephen has introduced me to a powerhouse attorney with a prominent law firm that's not connected to Advanced Tobacco Products. Both men listen as I tell them about the impossible position in which I find myself.

"We can't know for sure," the attorney says, "but I'm inclined to agree with you. The shareholders who called you may be planning a hostile takeover."

"I know one of those guys," Stephen adds. "And he's a hothead."

Stephen and the attorney have reconfirmed my worst fear. "So what are my options?"

"You could do a preemptive takeover," the attorney suggests. "That would avoid the company falling into outside hands. And if you had a seat on the board, the other shareholders should interpret that as a good thing. What's in your best interest is in their best interest. That's why they called you."

I don't know what I was expecting him to say, but this wasn't it. I'm trapped between a lion and a crocodile, and at the end of the day there's a chance I may anger and trigger one or both of them to bite me. I haven't recuperated from Jesse's rampage, and my kitchen cabinets still lay broken on the floor. Is it too much to ask for a few weeks without being trapped in the eye of a storm?

It's Thursday morning. Four days before my attorney and I go into Monday's annual shareholder meeting, and I'm holding a copy of the speech he's written for me to read when I call ATP's shareholders to solicit their votes. To be successful, I need to amass 51 percent of the shareholder votes, including my own.

"You're already the largest shareholder so more than likely," the attorney reminds me over the phone, "people will do what you think is best. Remember, you're limited to ten phone calls to collect the needed votes. That means if you call John Q. Shareholder, and he doesn't answer, that's one phone call. If you telephone John and leave a message on his answering machine, and he doesn't call you back, that's one phone call. If anyone challenges your actions, the SEC will do an audit, which means they'll subpoena your phone records. Stick to the rules, and you'll be fine."

What I'm about to do is not an inconsequential thing. Just the opposite, and I feel a huge responsibility to the company and its shareholders. Several times I've read aloud what I'm supposed to say, and I've thought about all the things that could go wrong, but there's no way I can predict something with which I have no experience.

I know all the largest shareholders personally, and I've decided to see if I can put together the votes without going to the group that called me two days ago. I don't want to be any part of whatever they might be planning, if anything. Instead, I start with the shareholder who helped bring in many of the original investors.

I dial the number and his executive assistant puts me right through. There's no turning back.

"Brenda Ray!" he says. "To what do I owe the pleasure?"

I ignore his greeting and begin reading word-for-word from the paper in my hand. "Hi George, this is Brenda Ray. I'm reading to you from a document prepared by my attorney, and I'm unable to say any more than what's written on this page." I pause for emphasis to let what I've said sink in.

"As you know, there's an Advanced Tobacco Products' shareholder meeting this coming Monday at the Menger Hotel in San Antonio, and I'd like to have your proxy so I can vote your shares should I need them." I pause and take a breath half expecting George to butt in, but he says nothing.

"I've become aware the company might be vulnerable to a group of shareholders who may—or may not—have our shares and our best interests at heart. As the single largest shareholder, I believe it's in everyone's best interest for me to be prepared to vote your shares if need be." I continue reading from the paper and when I reach the end I ask, "Will you give me your proxy to vote your shares?"

George is a savvy investor. He knows what's happening. Single-handedly, I'm preparing to do a hostile takeover of a public company.

"Yes. You have all of my votes."

George's easy *yes* is surprising, almost to the point of being alarming. It's the fuel I need to keep going. I thank him and call the next shareholder on my list and the next.

Not one shareholder says *no* to me or asks any questions, and by Friday afternoon I've met my goal. In fewer than ten phone calls, I've put together over 51 percent of the shareholder votes.

Monday morning most of the seats in the Menger Hotel's ornate Victorian ballroom are filled and buzzing with Advanced Tobacco Products' shareholders. Adjacent to the ballroom is the historic hotel bar where Teddy Roosevelt assembled the Rough

Riders to fight in the Spanish-American War. Somehow the location seems appropriate because I, too, have asked people here to take sides in what may be a war.

As my attorney and I walk through the crowd, there's a ripple effect of heads that turn and look in our direction. A few give me a quiet nod. If anyone recognizes the man I'm with, then they know he has a reputation for being a tough, take-no-prisoners litigator. We find two seats, three-quarters of the way to the back of the ballroom.

Advanced Tobacco Products' co-CEOs and their one board member are seated at a table in the front of the room, together with the company's attorney, who says, "Before we begin our scheduled shareholder meeting, I've been notified there's someone who'd like to speak."

That's my cue, and I stand up at my seat. Considering the magnitude of the situation, I'm strangely calm. Based on what I know, I'm doing the best for everyone concerned. As I begin to read from another document my attorney's prepared, I'm aware everyone in the room has turned in their seats to look at me.

When I get to "When I went to see management to ask about their plans for the company, one of the co-CEOs told me, 'It's none of your fucking business. What else do you want to know?'" there's an audible collective gasp from the people in the ballroom.

The two co-CEOs, the other board member, and their attorney abandon the scheduled agenda and leave the room to caucus, and when they return, they suggest to the shareholders that I should be appointed to the board of directors. It's the only move they could make. The devil you know is better than the devil you don't know, and in their eyes, right now I'm the devil. A shareholder vote is taken and passed. The annual meeting is concluded.

My attorney tells me I need to bring on another board member and a new CEO. I never wanted or thought I would be in this position. It's daunting, not something I would've chosen on my own. The group of shareholders who triggered my actions might've been blowing off steam, but I couldn't take that chance. I've embarrassed the two co-CEOs, both of whom are long-term friends, but the one who backed me into this impossible corner left me no choice.

This isn't a victory. It's more deaths, and I'm profoundly sad.

CHAPTER FORTY-FOUR

BOARD MEETINGS ARE COLD AND DISTANT. WE'RE warring factions stationed on opposite sides of the table, and the looks of contempt from the former co-CEOs have constructed a palpable wall between us. Once again I'm grieving the deaths of relationships, but instead of my husband they're friends from my already small social circle.

I won't be part of anymore backyard barbecues with Hatch chilies, potato salad, and carrot cake. I won't watch their children grow up, and there won't be any more vacations spent together. I'm a pariah, cut out of their lives forever. The only part of my heart that never had anything to fear has been ripped away and brutalized, and I imagine they're feeling the same way. All of us are experiencing betrayal in some way, and I fear they'll never be able to step into my shoes and understand.

I've brought in a new CEO and another board member, and the board voted to make me a paid management consultant; I cosign every check that goes out the door, and except for the financial pages, I write the annual shareholder letter as well as portions of every quarterly report sent to the shareholders.

The monthly consulting fee from ATP, together with Philip's Social Security, and the money I make from writing business plans, has given me a sliver of financial breathing room.

But more importantly, I know that no matter what happens, I will survive. I've weathered too many impediments to crawl under anyone's thumb ever again. It feels good to stand in my own power.

CHAPTER FORTY-FIVE

I'VE WRITTEN A BUSINESS PLAN FOR A NEW COMPANY I'VE started to produce technology-based curricula for elementary schools. An attorney has introduced me to a Dallas investment banker who might be interested in funding it. The attorney has dropped him off, and the plan is to have a short meeting at my house before I take him to the airport so he can catch a flight back to Dallas. I've made iced tea, and we're sitting on the black L-shaped sofa in my living room while I outline the company.

The investment banker nods as I play a prototype on a laser disc. "My business partner is with Harcourt Brace textbook publishers in Austin, and three of their curriculum developers are ready to come onboard with us. Last week I met with George Lucas's people at Skywalker Ranch about partnering with us."

"The *Star Wars* guy? Why doesn't he fund it?"

"They're not in the curriculum development business, plus they want a viable financial partner before they become involved."

"Your prototype is impressive. Who produced it?"

"I did. A curriculum developer and I wrote the script. I held a casting call and selected the children you saw, and the video was shot by a filmmaker I've worked with before."

The investment banker and I talk numbers, how much I'm

looking to raise, marketing, and when we expect to make a profit. He asks the usual questions. No curveballs or objections I can't overcome. When it's time to leave for the airport, he puts my business plan in his briefcase, and we stand up and walk toward the door.

He pauses and says, "I can help you put your deal together. I know some Dallas investors who might be interested." With one quick move, he leans down and puts his briefcase on the floor, then backs me up until I'm trapped between him and my front door. He leans into me and presses his body and his mouth against mine.

You presumptuous son-of-a-bitch! My anger meter skyrockets off the charts, but instead of grabbing his testicles, like I did Romeo's, I shove him off me and throw open the front door. I point toward the horizon on the other side of town. "The airport's that way." Then I hand him his briefcase and slam the door in his face.

The voice of the Neanderthal I'm no longer seeing plays in my head.

You shouldn't have been there in the first place.

I'm in my own home!

You shouldn't have been dressed that way.

I'm wearing a business suit!

The only other time I've closed the door in someone's face was the guy who hiked up the hill and told me we needed a bodyguard. With my binoculars, I'd watched him walk down the front steps, down the driveway, across Judson Road to the access road along the interstate. This time I don't need to watch the investment banker, because I'm confident he won't be back.

How is it I seem to attract assholes? I'd like to have a stable partner and a relationship with a good man. Philip was that man until the drugs and alcohol took over, but jerks like Jesse and the bozo investment banker who just left my house are no longer welcome in my life. I can make thousands of excuses why I was with Jesse, but the fact of the matter is I didn't want to be alone. I tolerated his narcissistic behavior and his womanizing. I should have ended the relationship long before I did, and that's on me, but from now on, I want to be able to spot the princes from the men who are nothing but charming.

The investment banker is standing at the end of my driveway with his briefcase in his hand. *I can help you put your deal together.* Seriously? You mean you were going to help yourself to a piece of me. Well, no thank you! I'm building a new Brenda, and if that means I'm single and a cashier at the Exxon station across the street then so be it, because I will never degrade myself by being with another man who uses me.

---·---

CHAPTER FORTY-SIX

"THAT GIRL WOULD'VE CHICKEN-FRIED HER TITS IF HE'D asked her to," says the man seated at a nearby table in this small-town Texas café. He and his friend are wearing overalls, scuffed work boots, and faded gimme caps with the name of their favorite Texas football team stitched across the front.

I ponder his curious remark because for longer than I care to admit, I was that girl. I did things, not because they were always what I wanted to do, but because they pleased a man.

His friend is digging into the meatloaf and mashed potato special. "She shoulda known he was up to no good," he says with his mouth full of sweet green peas. "A blind heifer coulda seen that one comin' round the water tank."

I feel sorry for the young woman they're talking about. Like me, perhaps she was confusing attention for love, or maybe she was afraid of what would happen if she said *no*.

The man at my table has reached out and taken my hand. "Don't be sittin' there, actin' like your Jimmy doesn't love you, because it only makes you look foolish."

It's not the first time he's said this to me. Sometimes he says it with a wry grin on his face, while other times, like now, he holds my gaze so I know he means it. I can feel his love. Like the men at the next table he's a Texas boy, but he has a higher regard for women. James Coffee comes from strong stock, and he was raised in a small West Texas town by a father who taught him to value and appreciate not only the land, but the women in his life as well.

I smile and let his large, warm hand envelop mine. Beginning with our first date, it was apparent to both of us that ours would be more than a casual passing relationship. Until then we'd each been mired in a toxic relationship where we'd stayed for all the wrong reasons. He's the only man I've known who's let his guard down and shared his heart, and in doing so, he's healed me in every way possible. I've waited all my life for James Coffee. He values God, family, and country—things that are somewhat new to me—and until I got to know James, I didn't know men like him existed.

James is an attorney, a man with a keen sense of humor, and he's proud of his Native American heritage. Today he's dressed in a nice shirt and a pressed pair of black jeans. His cowboy boots are polished, and his nails are manicured, but his hands are strong and callused from building fences and clearing brush. He knows where the center of the universe is and he's the real deal, a man of his word who's equally at home in small-town cafés as he is with billionaires or day laborers who don't speak English.

James says I was supposed to "class him up," but instead he's "dumbed me down"—a reference to how easy it is for me to slip into his West Texas twang—but I know it's part of his self-effacing humor. I've watched him in and out of the courtroom. He's smart and has a way of cutting to the heart of things without demeaning the other party. He's nourished the parts of me that were wounded, and for the first time in my life, I feel truly loved, valued, and appreciated, and in return, my heart is filled with unending love for him.

After we leave the café, James stops his truck near a riverbank in the rolling Texas Hill Country. As he shuts off the engine, I'm reminded of all the ways he shows me he loves me. Little things like the way he's made sure I can step out onto the pavement instead of into the high grass and weeds.

"Keep your bubble of awareness up, baby." It's his way of saying he wants me to be aware of my surroundings. "It looks kind of snaky here."

We get out of the truck and search for flat rocks he can skip across the river. The sun streams through the live oak trees, and I stand along the bank and watch as James sails stones across the water. He has a good arm and might have been a successful baseball pitcher, but he'd rather coach Little League. The stones skim and spin, leaving concentric circles as they dance across the surface. Each time they touch the glassy veneer, they send up little droplets of Morse Code. Dots and dashes that sparkle with promise and delight. As I watch him, I realize how content I am to be in the moment. I've told James everything, all of it, and I no longer have to pretend everything's all right because it is.

Since meeting James I've become a different person. I'm no longer drawn to men who are emotionally unavailable. Men who don't have my best interest at heart. I've stopped looking for the approval of the man in my life, and my self-esteem no longer comes from being with him. It comes from being a woman who will never again give my power away. And like Maya blue, the indestructible pigment on the pyramid in the jungle, I've emerged from the storms of the past ten years weathered and wiser, but I'm still here. I'm resilient, and each of my trials has come together to make me stronger. My voice is my power and holding firm to what's in my best interest is more important than trading it for the illusion of being loved. I am the woman life has made me. I'm my own person. Like me or not.

James has helped me see Mother in a different light. After

the first time he met her, he later said, "Poor woman. What must it be like to be in her skin?" While his observation was perceptive, it was his next comment that left an indelible mark on me. "She'll never be the mother you want, but you can be the daughter she needs," and he was right.

Mother's been diagnosed with dementia, and she needs me more than ever. I've researched dementia facilities and chosen one near me. It's someplace I'd want to be if I were in Mother's position, and I want to be there for her. Dementia has made her more difficult than usual, and that's saying a lot. Some days it's easier to be around her than others, but I don't want to have any regrets when she's no longer here.

Today, as I walk into her room, a nurse is standing next to her bed. The nurse has her arms up like she's trying to protect her face while Mother is yelling and swatting at her like she's a venomous flying insect.

"Is this your mother?" the woman asks me. Her voice is bathed in more than a hint of desperation. Mother leans forward in her bed, takes aim, and lands a hard punch on the nurse's arm. "We've been unable to take her temperature or her blood pressure, and we'd like to hook her up to a heart monitor, but we're all afraid of her."

Mother looks at me and then points at the nurse and hollers, "I don't trust her! She's trying to sell me something! You never know about people who just walk into your apartment uninvited!"

When I tell her the woman is a nurse who's trying to help her, Mother picks up a cup full of water and throws it at me. "Well, now she can help you!"

I laugh and brush off the water. "Mom, the nurse needs to connect some electrodes to the sticky pads they've already placed on your chest."

"Well, you do what you want with yours, and I'll do what I want with mine!" With that, Mother begins tearing off the adhesive pads from her body and proceeds to line them up, one by one, in a straight line along the top of her other arm.

Sometimes I wish I could take Mother and go back in time to when she was a little girl in Tennessee. I would tell her she's just as worthy and important as the other little girls who didn't grow up poor. The ones with pretty clothes, whose parents weren't divorced. I would kneel beside her and tell her how special she is. How there's nothing she needs to feel ashamed about.

Then I'd take the girl by the hand and turn up the music and dance with her in the middle of the room. And when I saw a faint glint in her eyes, a recognition of the woman she could become, I'd step back and let her dance in her own light. And in that first unsure moment, when she wanted to retreat once more to the shadows, I would lead her back into the light and tell her to trust herself.

"Everything's going to be all right. You're meant to be here."

"So often in life, things that you regard as an impediment turn out to be great, good fortune."

—RUTH BADER GINSBURG

AFTERWORD

Maya Blue is the culmination of decades of keeping huge parts of my life a secret from everyone except a small handful of people. Writing this book has been one of my most gut-wrenching experiences and, at the same time, it's helped me see everyone involved in a new light, especially myself.

The Big Chief tablet with the red cover I bought in Belize allowed me to document my bus ride from Belize City to where the driver let me out on the side of the road. After the children went back to their seats, I opened the tablet and began writing down everything around me: the interior of the bus, and my fellow travelers, including Mr. Rooster, along with the music that was playing over the loudspeakers. I've written about them just as they were, and in my mind, I can see everything as though I'm looking at a photograph. Once Estéban picked me up in his taxi, I never wrote another word in my tablet, but I will continue to see jolting images of that day for as long as I live.

Since my mid-twenties, I've kept calendars that also served as diaries, and during the Advanced Tobacco Products days, I kept a journal. After I bought my first Apple computer I began making notes about the people and events in this book.

In 2019 I began writing *Maya Blue* full-time. As I explained to the amazing readers of my blog, I needed to step away from blogging to work on my memoir. A blog and a memoir require different writing voices and muscles, and I couldn't do both at the same time.

Much of this book was written during 2020 while we were all isolated during the first year of COVID-19. For me, two terrifying things were taking place: the stress and fear of a new disease the world knew little about, while some of the worst moments of my life poured out of me onto my keyboard.

When I sat down to write this book, I decided to start with what I sometimes think of as my "involuntary time in the jungle." Over the years it's been easier for me to think about Guatemala this way as opposed to being taken at gunpoint. I thought if I could write about what happened in the jungle I could write about anything, but I was wrong. Writing about how Philip got off track and I surrendered my voice was much harder. I didn't expect that to be the case, and I struggled for the next two years to get my feelings down on the page.

Several years ago, I was on a panel at Internet Week in New York City with the editor-in-chief of the now-shuttered *More* magazine. Later I called her to say I wanted to be part of *More's* upcoming Reinvention Convention. Her only response was, "Do you have any experience reinventing yourself?" While it was a valid question, I nearly fell off my chair with laughter.

Nothing I've been through is funny, and I realize many people have been through worse things, but looking back I should have said: "Do you mean *after* my husband died and left me with little money, three years' back taxes—penalties and interest—a million dollars' worth of cancer bills, a balloon note due on my home, and no insurance or death benefit on the mortgage? *After* I was taken at gunpoint in Guatemala? *After* I singlehandedly did a hostile takeover of a public company in four days? Then there's what happened *after* Guatemala. After I relinquished my power. Again."

Nothing could have prepared me for the violence in the jungle, but I believe my life experiences up until then made me better able to survive it. I was also lucky. Incredibly lucky. Since then, I've found Internet references to the same commando group that took me. Savage soldiers who are feared above all others. Known for gang-raping pregnant women then strangling or beheading them, cutting the fetuses from their bodies, and then bashing their unborn children against concrete pillars and throwing their still-alive mothers-to-be down the water wells of their villages.

The United Nations estimates that between 1960 and 1996, 200,000 people were murdered and 45,000 *Los Desaparecidos,* "the disappeared," were killed by the Guatemalan military and the group that took me. According to the United Nations, the 1980s, when I was taken, were the years of the worst atrocities. I have deep compassion for the people of Guatemala because for one afternoon and a thousand nightmares since then, I got a glimpse of what it was like to live there.

In 1987, Advanced Tobacco Products, Inc. sold the smokeless cigarette patents in Philip Ray's name to pharmaceutical giant Pharmacia Leo. Pharmacia redesigned FAVOR® to look less like a cigarette and more like a medical device. Pharmacia named it the Nicotrol® Inhaler, a smoking cessation aid, and it became part of the Nicorette®/Nicotrol® family of products which included the nicotine patch and the nicotine gum. A negotiated percentage of the royalties from the worldwide sales of the Nicotrol® Inhaler were paid in the form of dividends to ATP shareholders. In 2003, ATP became a wholly owned subsidiary of IVAX Pharmaceuticals, a multinational pharmaceutical company. ATP shareholders received IVAX Pharmaceuticals stock in exchange for their shares of ATP common stock. These business decisions benefited all of ATP's shareholders, including me, and helped me pay off the debts Philip left me.

In his 1996 *60 Minutes* interview with Mike Wallace, Dr. Jeffrey Wigand, former vice president of Research and Development at Brown & Williamson Tobacco Corporation, blew the whistle on an industry that not only knew nicotine was addicting, but intentionally added known carcinogenic and addictive chemicals to their tobacco blends to increase the effects of nicotine.

The *60 Minutes* interview revealed that Brown & Williamson had privately acknowledged "cigarettes are a delivery device for nicotine," but for liability reasons, senior management—together with their staff attorney—purged all references about making a safer cigarette. They also hid documents that could be used against the company in lawsuits brought against them by sick and dying smokers.

In the same interview, Dr. Wigand revealed he'd received serious death threats, his children received death threats, he and his family had bodyguards, and subsequently the stress was too great and he and his wife divorced. His reputation and career were deliberately ruined to discredit him. Mike Moore, then-Attorney General of Mississippi, said he feared for Wigand's life because the tobacco industry had "perpetrated the biggest fraud on the American public in history . . . They have killed millions and millions of people and made a profit on it."

Since Philip was also making cocaine, I realize the intruders and the threats we received could have come from another source. However, the ordeal Dr. Jeffrey Wigand and his family endured reconfirmed that what happened to me and Philip was not perpetrated by someone who'd been "playing a prank."

While Philip's smokeless cigarette, FAVOR®, had nicotine in it, and nicotine is addictive, it never killed anyone, unlike the 2,000 carcinogens and by-products of burning found in traditional cigarettes. FAVOR® did, however, threaten the United States government's second-largest revenue source—the tax on cigarettes—along with the loss of billions of dollars in cigarette sales to the six largest tobacco companies in the world. It's why our legal experts predicted, "They won't let you get away with it." FAVOR® underscored what the federal government and the big tobacco companies wanted to remain hidden.

The current vapes and e-cigarettes bear no resemblance to FAVOR® Smokeless Cigarettes. Since nicotine is capable of vaporizing all by itself, the nicotine in FAVOR® didn't need to be activated by heat, as it is in today's e-cigs, and while FAVOR® looked like a cigarette, users didn't have to light it and didn't need a battery. They simply inhaled the nicotine vapor, and there was no annoying vapor or smoke like there is in today's e-cigs.

There are several things I hope history will remember about Jon Philip Ray. Yes, he got off track with his project downstairs, but addiction can happen to anyone. Philip Ray was a good man. A brilliant man. But more than anything, Philip Ray made one of the most important, groundbreaking contributions the world will ever know: He conceived of, and developed, the first personal computer along with the first computer on a chip we now call the microprocessor.

History should also know there are others who, at every opportunity, continue to rewrite this history and take credit for many of Philip Ray's achievements, as well as those of the original hardware and software engineers of Computer Terminal Corporation—subsequently renamed Datapoint Corporation—including *everything* I'm about to outline in the next few paragraphs.

Their claims about the history of the first personal computer are very different from my firsthand knowledge and recollections about those early days as well as those of the original Computer Terminal/Datapoint employees. I cannot stand by and let these people rewrite the history of one of the biggest contributions to not just the computer world, but to the advancement of almost every facet of life in every country in the world.

Here are the facts: the real story of the first personal computer. It is well documented by Computer Terminal Corporation/Datapoint Corporation annual reports, countless business magazine and newspaper articles including *The Wall Street Journal*, and an audio tape interview Philip Ray gave shortly before he died to business reporter Richard Erickson.

In 1968, Jon Philip Ray and his business partner, Austin (Gus) O. Roche, came out of the space industry at a time when technology was advancing at a rapid pace. Together with input from Dr. Bob McClure, a computer consultant and teaching assistant when Philip was a student at the University of Texas, Phil and Gus conceptualized and developed a desktop computer terminal. Their brainchild was compact and had a glass display screen and a keyboard. It replaced the noisy Model 33 teletype machines that connected to the giant computer mainframes of the day which were the backbone of the booming computer time-sharing market. They named it the Datapoint 3300.

Together, Philip Ray and Gus Roche wrote the business plan they used to raise startup capital. Philip drew and hand-lettered thirteen large poster boards that detailed the current market and its projected growth, as well as the product development of their new terminal. On another poster board, Philip's older brother, an architect at the time, drew and hand-colored a sketch of what this revolutionary computer terminal might look like. Philip carried these poster boards on airplanes and to investor meetings in a zippered brown leather double-elephant folio.

Philip Ray and Gus Roche are the *only* founders of Computer Terminal Corporation/Datapoint Corporation, and from the moment they came together as a team, Phil and Gus—and no one else—envisioned another terminal which became the company's second product, the Datapoint 2200. It was designed to be a "smart," stand-alone desktop computer—the personal computer.

The Datapoint 2200 has since been researched and authenticated by the Institute of Electrical and Electronics Engineers (IEEE) and named as the first desktop personal computer. Philip Ray's and Gus Roche's achievements have profoundly changed the world, as did Johannes Gutenberg's moveable-type printing press, Henry Ford's Model T automobile, and Thomas Edison's lightbulb.

In 2004, eight years after James Coffee and I were married, I was diagnosed with estrogen-positive breast cancer. I had ten breast cancer surgeries and eight rounds of chemo. At the time, it was difficult to find the answers to questions such as "Could the ingredients in the creams and makeup I put on my body, or the foods I eat, contribute to a recurrence of my breast cancer?" and "How do I deal with painful sex caused by cancer treatment?" As a result, I started what was repeatedly voted the Top Breast Cancer Blog on the Internet.

Just as I'd done with many of the other things in my life, I used my skills to research informative blog topics, interview scientists, high-profile people, and top organizations in the breast cancer community, and I produced over one hundred videos for patients, caregivers, husbands, and children. I became the girlfriend who talked about everything—things doctors are often uncomfortable discussing—and I spoke at numerous groups around the country including Yahoo's Fortune 100, invitation-only event during Internet Week in New York City.

On Christmas 2010, my darling James died unexpectedly of cardiac arrest while out for a walk. Grieving his loss is the most difficult thing I've ever experienced. A few years later, I decided I no longer wanted to write exclusively about cancer. I wanted to share my wealth of varied experience with women over fifty, and I started 1010PARKPLACE.COM, which I'm proud to say has been repeatedly voted a "Top 10 Blog" for this demographic.

And the Spy House on the Hill? I sold it to the developer who owned the adjacent land. He thought the best use of my property would be as a parking lot for a car dealership. He tore down the house, one of the most historic properties in San Antonio, but died before he could finish his plan of excavating the highest hill in the city. The brick wall around the car park still stands, but the sundae is now minus the cherry on top.

As I drove down the driveway—for the last time—I passed under the canopy of post oak trees, through the locked gate that had failed to protect me. I never turned around to look at the house I'd loved as though it were a living, breathing being. The house I'd once told Philip, "You'll have to carry me out of here in a pine box."

Instead, I got on the freeway and headed in a different direction, to the place James and I bought in the Texas Hill Country. I carried with me the steel-like threads that have been a part of my core since the day I was born.

In writing this book, I've been forced to open the box of toxic secrets I've kept hidden in my emotional closet, and by giving voice to them, I've freed myself from the power they held over me. For most of my life, I pretended to be afraid of nothing and no one, and in the end, I learned we are what we pretend to be. Now I know there are no limits to my strength, and I can get through anything.

I've realized that surviving life's storms is often more important than the storms themselves, and when they're over, we need to get up and regroup the best way we know how and continue to charge at life again and again. Anything less isn't living. Like the hashtags #makelifecount and #whatareyouwaitingfor, which I created for my website 1010PARKPLACE.COM and my @1010PARKPLACE Instagram account, these are the only paths forward that make any sense to me.

ACKNOWLEDGMENTS

Memoir is my favorite genre to read, and I send gratitude to my favorite memoir authors whose well-dogeared books line the shelves behind my desk. In no particular order, they are Cheryl Strayed, Adrienne Brodeur, Patti Smith, Tembi Locke, Frances Mayes, Mary Karr, Dani Shapiro, Lee & Bob Woodruff, Jeannette Walls, Laura Munson, Linda Sivertsen, Elizabeth Gilbert, Amy Bloom, Keith Richards, Robbie Robertson, Jann Wenner, Bill Clegg, Sandra Cisneros, Doreen M. McGettigan, Joan Didion, Rich Cohen, Nora Ephron, Amanda Lindhout and her coauthor Sara Corbett, Stanley Tucci, Natasha Trethewey, Rick Bragg, Sting, Amaryliss Fox, and Anthony Bourdain.

I owe a big thank you to the readers of my blog, 1010-PARKPLACE.COM, who for years have loved me and encouraged me to write this book. As one reader wrote, "We want to know what your life was like before you came to us." Numerous times readers have asked how I've survived the things life has put in my path like breast cancer and the unexpected death of my second husband, James; how I've managed to remain so strong and upbeat. They knew nothing about what I've written in this memoir. As I said in one of my blog posts, surviving was a conscious decision, not by faking it, but by doing the necessary work to recuperate from whatever took me down. It wasn't easy, but my mother and my first husband, Philip, were motivating examples of what could happen to me if I did nothing to save myself or I chose the wrong path.

I send my thanks to Esther Zimmer, writer, blogger, friend, and self-awareness truth seeker who traveled from her home in London to Paris to meet me, a woman she knew only through my blogs. Esther was the one who planted the seed for me to write this book with her insightful comment, "If these are the stories you're willing to share with us, what are the ones you haven't told us?" I'm an adrenaline junkie, and by most standards, some of the first person stories I share on my blog are far outside the norm. But as you can tell, dear Essie, there was a lot I was keeping from almost everybody. Secrets that stayed buried until you helped me see it was time to dig them up.

My thanks to Debra Shriver, former media executive at Hearst Media and published author of two beautiful books about Paris and New Orleans, who was the first person to read my manuscript. I seem to remember Deb called me at something like 4:30 in the morning and said, "Hey, you, in the Wonder Woman cuffs! This book is going to catch on fire!" I was apprehensive about what she might say, or find a nice way *not* to say, but her encouragement bolstered me and kept me going.

I'm indebted to my dear friend Daniel Casanova, who refused to hear all the reasons why I should stop writing and abandon my attempts to get published. He kept me focused on the finish line, which is the book you're now holding in your hands. Thank you, Daniel. I love you.

I'm grateful to Laura Munson, *New York Times* and *USA Today* bestselling author and founder of the Haven Writing Programs who opened doors for me, taught me how to lay out a map for my book, and how to write in scenes. Laura worked with me on several drafts, encouraging me when I didn't "get it," and cheering for me when I finally understood the nuances of becoming more self-aware and transparent on the page. Except for when I wrote a sentence here and a paragraph there, I'm sure there were times she felt frustrated with me because I wasn't taking her advice. On the final draft, Laura left me a comment that said, "This was a complete pleasure to read and behold, Brenda. I think you're there." I cried when I read it.

Thank you, sweet lady, for hanging in there with me and making me a better writer. I love you.

My love and gratitude to Linda Sivertsen, also known as the "Book Mama," author, ghostwriter, and coauthor of eleven books including two *New York Times* bestsellers, TedTalk alumnus, host of the top-rated Beautiful Writers Podcast and the Beautiful Writers retreat in Carmel, teacher, and friend. Linda opened doors for me, taught me how to write a book proposal, and encouraged me when I was overwhelmed. Like me, Linda is a woman who perseveres no matter what. She's surrounded by magic and has the inside scoop on when the moon will be in retrograde. Thank you for your wise words and your friendship.

Thank you to the amazing Betsy Rapoport, former executive editor at Random House, writer, ghostwriter, and brilliant storysmith who worked with me through several versions of the manuscript. Like Laura Munson, Betsy told me I needed to be more transparent with my feelings, good and bad. During one of our conversations, she said "I needed to strangle myself more," an exaggerated but image-provoking line she'd borrowed from another Random House editor. And just when I thought I was almost there, Betsy encouraged me to "kill some of my darlings," my best chapters, and write what turned out to be five new ones. This book is much stronger because of you, Betsy. I adore you.

I send my gratitude to my fellow members of the Haven I Writer's Retreat in Whitefish, Montana, who listened and supported me as I read them a few passages from a memoir I was thinking of writing. As it turns out, I'm saving those for another memoir. My love and thank you to Lee Baker and Becca Mai, my fellow Haven II writers who read every word of my manuscript and offered me solid, well-thought-out critiques and encouragement while we read one another's work during our many COVID-19 Zoom calls. Without fail, Lee and Becca found the holes and flaws and the parts I should have written about in more detail. Everyone who's a writer should be in a trusted writers' group. Don't join a group of writers who just smile and nod politely about what you've written. Find fellow writers who make you better at your craft as you do the same for them.

To Beth Davey, my literary agent, who steadfastly stayed with me as the entire publishing industry changed around us and memoir became a hard sell. From the beginning, Beth loved and believed in my manuscript and encouraged me throughout the entire publishing process. She continues to be a trusted advisor. I appreciate, love, and value you, Beth. Thank you.

My love and gratitude to my fellow "Carmelies" as Linda Sivertsen calls us, members of her Beautiful Writers Retreat in Carmel, who have since become my lifelong friends: Grace Kraaijvanger, writer and founder of The Hivery in San Francisco, dedicated to creating the next chapter of your life; Laticia Diane Carter, the profoundly talented, bring-me-to-my-knees writer, songwriter, and certified spiritual life coach; and Joanne Socha, writer, boutique luxury travel designer at Travel Far & Well, and my cheerleader supreme at every turn in the road of this journey.

And to Doreen McGettigan, longtime friend, blogger, writing and publishing coach, and twice-published author who read my first draft and assured me I would get an agent. Thank you! I needed your encouragement.

My gratitude and thanks to everyone at She Writes Press,

especially the brilliant, inimitable publisher at She Writes Press and SparkPress, Brooke Warner. Brooke has carved out a new award-winning hybrid publishing paradigm that includes book distribution by Simon & Schuster. She's a wealth of knowledge about the publishing industry. Brooke, I thank you for all your support and help as you've juggled a thousand other books and balls in addition to mine. Thank you for selecting my memoir to be published. As we say in Texas, I'm forever beholden.

Thank you to Lauren Wise, my project manager; to editor Anne Durette who made my words and punctuation sparkle and who caught several key areas that needed to be changed; and to Tabitha Lahr for taking my Polaroid SX-70 photograph and turning it into a beautiful book cover.

I send my appreciation and gratitude to superstar publicist Emi Battaglia, for putting my manuscript in front of the right people and media outlets. And to Susie Stangland, internet and social media wizard for guiding my digital steps. You're both amazing!

I value and appreciate every one of you who's helped me make this a better book, although thank you seems like a small acknowledgment for the huge roles you've played in bringing my book to print.

XOXOX,
Brenda

ABOUT THE AUTHOR

Credit: Jennifer Denton

BRENDA COFFEE is a published writer, photographer, and filmmaker with a BA in journalism and film. An avid adventurer, dynamic speaker, and successful businesswoman, she was managing consultant and board member of a public company she sold to Big Pharma. Coffee is the creator of two Top 10 websites, including 1010PARKPLACE.COM, home to her popular BRENDA'S BLOG, which delivers candid information about finances, fashion, life, and relationships to the wealthiest, best-educated, most powerful demographic in history: women over 50. She resides in Texas.

Looking for your next great read?

We can help!

Visit www.shewritespress.com/next-read
or scan the QR code below for a list
of our recommended titles.

She Writes Press is an award-winning
independent publishing company founded to
serve women writers everywhere.